I Shop, Therefore I Am

Also by Mary Portas

Windows: The Art of Retail Display
Shop Girl: A Memoir
Work Like a Woman: A Manifesto for Change
Rebuild: How to thrive in the new Kindness Economy

I Shop, Therefore I Am

The '90s, Harvey Nicks, and me

Mary Portas

CANONGATE

First published in Great Britain in 2025
by Canongate Books Ltd, 14 High Street, Edinburgh EH1 1TE

canongate.co.uk

2

Extract from 'style' by Charles Bukowski from *Mockingbird Wish Me Luck* is reproduced
with the permission of the publisher, Ecco, an imprint of HarperCollins US.

The poem 'Come to the Edge' by Christopher Logue from *Selected Poems* is reproduced
with the permission of the publisher, Faber & Faber.

British Library Cataloguing-in-Publication Data
A catalogue record for this book is available on
request from the British Library

ISBN 9781837264414

Typeset in Bembo Std by Palimpsest Book Production Ltd,
Falkirk, Stirlingshire

Printed and bound by CPI Group (UK) Ltd, Croydon CR0 4YY

The manufacturer's authorised representative in the EU for product safety is
Authorised Rep Compliance Ltd, 71 Lower Baggot Street, Dublin D02 P593 Ireland
(arccompliance.com)

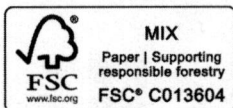

MIX
Paper | Supporting
responsible forestry
FSC
www.fsc.org
FSC® C013604

To the shopkeepers – who rise each morning with quiet
determination and hope in their hearts.
Because of you, the world outside our front doors
feels a little more like home.
This is for you – with gratitude and awe.

Contents

CONTENTS

Disclaimer

R ETAIL IS MORE THAN JUST a business – it is a stage where
personalities, ambitions and human connections play out in
a way that is both exhilarating and unpredictable. My journey at
Harvey Nichols was no exception. It was a career filled with
extraordinary people, unforgettable moments and lessons that
shaped not only my professional life but also my perspective on
business, leadership, resilience and the art of retail itself.

This book is a true reflection of that journey. While the events
and emotions are deeply real, the characters you will meet along
the way are, in some ways, not. They are an amalgamation of the
talented, brilliant and sometimes challenging individuals I encoun-
tered throughout my career. Their names and identities have been
reimagined, but their essence – their impact on me and on the
business – remains very much intact.

I hope that as you read, you find joy in these stories, just as I
found joy (and sometimes chaos) in living them. I hope you see
the passion, the challenges and the triumphs that come with

working at the heart of a world-renowned luxury retailer. Most of all, I want to thank the real incredible people – the directors, the business heads and the teams that made it all happen. They were an extraordinary bunch, and I will always be grateful for the years I spent working alongside them.

So step into my world of retail, where truth and storytelling intertwine. It's a journey worth taking.

M.P.

June 2025

Introduction

An afternoon at Harvey Nicks

Autumn 1994

W E'RE FIVE MINUTES AWAY FROM curtains up on the catwalk
show that kick-starts London Fashion Week and there's no
sign of Naomi Campbell – the model who'll make or break this
monumental gamble. As has become customary in my career at
Harvey Nichols, the dowager department store we've taken from
faded to high fashion in five years, I've taken a punt on doing
something that could be legendary – or a disaster. Everyone from
the UK fashion industry is crammed into the fifth-floor restaurant,
knocking back one more mimosa before they must take their seats.
I spot British *Vogue* Editor-in-Chief Alexandra Shulman chatting
to a stylist who's been calling my team all week complaining about
her second-row seat. We've refused to move her. There is a strict
hierarchy of seating: editors-in-chiefs and fashion directors front

row, stylists second, and assistants so far back all they'll see are the Philip Treacy hats. Mind you, those alone are worth the trip. The stylist had tried every threat imaginable – 'I'll pull your looks from my *A Night at the Museum* pre-fall shoot,' she trilled – but my team has stuck to their plan, fearing one capitulation will lead to a tsunami of demands. Still, she's come. As have the buying teams from America's leading department stores, Barneys and Bergdorf, all flashy smiles and splashy budgets.

By giving the new voices of British fashion a platform, New Gen was designed to prove that Harvey Nichols is no longer a department store selling cashmere and quilts. It is a fashion destination for a newly emerging customer who wants glamour and grit. It's done just that, while also providing a welcome injection of cash and publicity to struggling designers.

But this season, we've gone rogue. Harvey Nichols has just become a household name, thanks to a starring role in BBC primetime show *Absolutely Fabulous*. A satirical look at the fashion industry through the eyes of Patsy and Edina, played by Joanna Lumley and Jennifer Saunders, it has managed a rare feat: winning over both the masses and industry insiders. And, by giving the actors a free rein to film (and shop) in the store, 'Harvey Nicks' has become a character itself, which is why we've decided to work with Jennifer Saunders, to spoof our own New Gen show. Betty Jackson has designed a collection of T-shirt dresses, underwear, bodysuits and tank tops, emblazoned with now-famous slogans from the show. 'I'm chanting as we speak' is the one I've got my eye on. You'll be able to buy them in Harvey Nicks tomorrow. If we get through the next few hours.

Backstage, a team of dressers – no-nonsense women in their sixties, who are more interested in stitching than star-spotting, are helping the models into T-shirts and PVC trousers. In the corner is the bridal outfit Naomi Campbell will wear for the finale – only, there is no Naomi, and I am now getting skittish.

Desmond, a brilliant member of my design team who has styled the show, hands me a glass of champagne. 'I know you hate the stuff,' he says. 'But trust me, it's like angels pissing down on your tongue. So get it down you and relax.'

And then, *finally*, the clatter of my assistant Bean, who has risked a heart attack to run up six flights of metal steps to tell me that, 'She's arrived!' I am grateful for my flat shoes – the ones I usually keep under my desk for meetings with the managing director, a short man who I feel is always looking for something to use against me – as I trot down to meet Naomi. 'Oh, I love doing silly things like this,' she giggles as I air-kiss her hello, her girlish voice defying a face that is so statuesque it looks like it's been carved out of a single piece of marble. Des is styling her in a tight white T-shirt with 'Fash Mag Slag' written in sequins across it, white Calvin Klein briefs, a big gold Cherry Chau tiara and masses of white tulle tied around her with a grosgrain ribbon. She's our camped-up version of the fashion bride that traditionally ends all couture catwalk shows – a bid for business from designers who need big-budget bridal commissions to keep their houses afloat. As Des talks her through it, Naomi laughs and strips naked. Then she transforms into Naomi, the supermodel, wordlessly letting the dresser drape the silk tulle just so before striding around the room to practise her walk.

Meanwhile, Jennifer Saunders is front of house, introducing the show in her laconic fashion. 'This season I was inspired by neutrals, and more neutrals with a touch of more neutrally neutrals mixed in.' As the first models step out, wearing '100% sweetie darling' slogan T-shirts and swinging PVC bags that might as well be bin bags, there's a lightbulb moment as the audience suddenly get it. Then it's Naomi time. As she sweeps on for the finale, flanked by a Bolly-swigging Joanna Lumley, trying to flounce the wedding train, Saunders scoffs: 'This one can't walk, Pats.' There's a moment of silence. Naomi refuses to carry on until the song from her new album *Love And Tears* is played. It's unclear if she's playing up to her character or just too astute to miss a promo opportunity. But by the time the chorus hits, the audience are in hysterics, and my team are popping champagne backstage. In the melee afterwards, Naomi saunters up to Des, then bends down to plant a kiss on his cheek. 'Thanks, darling, that was fun,' she coos, leaving my team smitten. As for me? I'm already onto the next idea . . .

FIVE YEARS EARLIER

We're a long way from Watford

Spring 1989

OXBLOOD VELVET CURTAINS FRAME THE shop windows looking out onto Sloane Street. They're pinned and draped in such a way that your eye is drawn to the pair of Rayne green satin slingbacks sitting atop a neoclassical-style plaster plinth. Only I'm looking at the dead flies on the rug below, wondering why no one from the team has been in to vacuum the windows before the shop opens in thirty minutes' time. My team, I should say. Because today I start as Head of Visual Merchandising and Store Design at Harvey Nichols – the first woman to take up the role. That means that this ten-foot window will now be mine. Along with – I count them – the three, four, five, six . . . fuck me, twenty-seven windows I see as I walk around the shop to the staff entrance.

It's 1989, I'm twenty-eight and about to enter the world of luxury fashion – a space that, although alien to me, instinctively appeals. Department stores are still considered the pinnacle of visual merchandising. Unlike individual boutiques, we have acres of windows and a curious, heady mix of fashion, beauty, accessories and even interiors to showcase. The balance of what and how to display these is a creative's dream. I stop and stand back to take it all in, those cavernous windows to refit with audacious ideas every eight weeks or less. This will be my stage.

I'd asked my sister Tish to get the same train as me that first day. Tish is the clinical editor of *The Nursing Times*, a newspaper that publishes out of an office behind a curry house on the Euston Road, so she's used to this journey. I'd spent the previous evening rifling through a pile of Topshop suits to try and find something to wear that said Lady Di rather than Cyndi Lauper, but I now realise the fluorescent orange shoulder-padded skirt suit isn't exactly subtle. The few women in our carriage in the sea of men are legal assistants or secretaries for accountants, wearing mid-calf skirts and trainers. They'll change into heels at their desk.

Tish and I sit together, nervously looking out for abandoned bags that'll prompt a message over the tannoy about security. The recent spate of IRA bomb threats has everyone jumpy.

'How are you feeling?' she asks gently.

I tell her what I know about Harvey Nichols. 'Harrods has all the money. Big budgets, zingy ideas, pots of dosh. Makes a fortune with the international market coming to ogle and spend,' I say. 'We're like the ageing dowager duchess down the end of the road living in the smaller property where the curtains are frayed and the china is chipped.'

I explain that I've been recruited to create window displays that will get the place talked about. Many big American stores are doing the 'experience thing' and it's working. Management needs new ideas to get new customers through the revolving doors and spending.

'Ideas I can do,' I confess. 'It's the people I'm worried about.'

I've been put in the sales team. My boss told me at the interview he loved working with feisty women. 'Just not as much as I love my wife,' he added, laughing. 'Unbelievable taste, unbelievable friends.' He was joking. I think. Still, the only other woman I know of in management is the Fashion Director, a woman called Antonia Allard, who was so scarily fashionable that all of the editors looked to her for inspiration.

'Then there's my display team. Eighteen of them, most of whom will probably be my age,' I tell her. 'Do I look like I'm qualified to be a boss?'

'Well, you've never had much trouble bossing us all around,' she quips, taking my hand. She teases me about my gothic painted nails but I don't mind because I know that, secretly, she's proud I've found my place.

'Just remember what Mum would say,' she says as she ushers me off the train and towards the bus stop to catch the 390 to Victoria.

I think of what Mum often told me. 'You, my darling, are already enough just as you are. Hold your head high, not because you're better than anyone else, but because you owe it to see the horizon fully and claim your space in the world.'

As always, she was right.

IN THE PAST

Packed nothing but hope

The 1970s

Growing up, I never felt I fitted into any of the existing systems of society. When it came to school, I just couldn't pay attention to what they wanted me to — only if a subject or a teacher excited me. But in a convent run by nuns, that was bloody rare. I wasn't interested in their intrinsic motivation of getting good grades, then getting a good job. Merit-badge mentality has never been my thing. I never had a best friend. I would fly in and out of different cohorts, boring easily and getting distracted.

Home was the same. I was the noisy one, pushing boundaries. I was fourth out of five and hated the fact that I had no real status. I wasn't the eldest, nor the first girl or the adored youngest. The eldest was my brother Michael, who each year without fail won the best student award. My big sister Tish was much the same. Compliant and studious. Mum was fiercely proud of them both. Next came Joe, the gentle dreamy creative who could draw

9

and read books well above most school kids' reading level. And then my little brother Lawrence, who was so beautiful and loving that all of us used to grab him and kiss him endlessly. I often led him astray. He would follow me, five or six steps behind, copying whatever nonsense and naughtiness I decided to do. No matter what rules my mother put in place, I broke them. I loved and respected her, but just couldn't be that kid who made her proud.

But when my imagination and interest were awakened, you couldn't stop me. In fact, I would border on being obsessive, with a very short fuse if people weren't delivering at the speed and commitment I was. That's how I was when I discovered theatre. Plays. Literature. Art. I didn't just act in them. I wrote them, designed the scenery, cast them and made the sets. Rehearsed weekends and late nights while my pals were out clubbing . . . And then charged people to see them – knowing they were worth it. Somehow in this wonderful world, where make-up, lights, music, storytelling, costumes and performance came together in a trans-formative alchemy, I could feel myself come alive. So, with school nearing its end, I started applying to drama schools and univer-sities. I had found my thing.

I was always hungry for more, but then life stopped abruptly. By the time I was nineteen, I'd lost both my parents. Mum died suddenly. She'd always been so sharp that when she started to get confused, we knew something wasn't right. The doctors dismissed it as 'The Change', prescribing her antidepressants like they had so many other women of a certain age. We weren't to indulge her, they said, by letting her languish in bed. A week later she was in a coma in a hospital bed. We were told she had meningitis, then encephalitis – a diagnosis no amount of rosary beads or Hail Marys could overcome.

It was as if the world had turned the lights off. Home, once a place of safety, comfort and crazy family life, became hollow and alien. Each morning, I left the house crying, only stopping when I stepped onto the school bus. On the way home, I'd start again. I returned to an empty, unbearable silence. My elder siblings had already left home – Tish to study nursing at UCH, Michael to university and Joe to start a hairdressing apprenticeship. It wasn't fair to expect them to come back to a place that emitted sadness. A place where my father sat in the front room in darkness, listening to Josef Locke records on a loop. The Irish tenor could never quite cover his sobbing.

I learnt how to run a household, stretching the weekly budget with on-the-turn produce the local greengrocers would add to what used to be my mum's regular order. 'A little bit extra, my love,' they'd say, kindly. 'Use those courgettes today, mind. They'll bulk up any stew.' If I had a play to rehearse for, Lawrence would cobble together dinner. The rest of the time, I was in charge. At seventeen, I was learning to navigate adult grief with the vulner-ability of a teenager, struggling to find my way through.

My father couldn't cope alone. It had always been my mum who'd held the family together. Dad tried to learn, but the bulk of the domestic burden fell to me. Things I didn't even know I didn't know soon hit me: if you could refreeze defrosted minced lamb; when to flip the mattress. My father had always been a

11

workaholic, so perhaps I shouldn't have been surprised that he buried himself in work, or the Widows and Widowers Club in West Watford. Within eighteen months he'd met a widow in her fifties with too much perfume, too much hair dye and not enough kindness. The same day they sat us down to tell us they were marrying, all I could focus on was the Mr Kipling fondant fancies Dad had given me a few extra coins to get in for tea. I was shut down and in denial.

Nine months into their marriage, my father died of a massive heart attack, found slumped over his desk one morning. His new wife inherited everything and she turfed us all out. Not one of us remembers packing up and leaving. There was an almost surreal detachment where our hearts just couldn't process the loss. We were orphans. And homeless. I had no place to go. Not knowing where I'd end up, all I took was those of Mum's belongings that I could carry, wrapped carefully in tissue paper in my suitcase: her statue of Saint Theresa, a battered recipe book and her Christmas cake decorations.

Grief

'I SAT WITH MY ANGER long enough until she told me her real name was grief': these words, often attributed to C. S. Lewis, resonate with me. Certainly, while grieving Dad, I felt angry and betrayed. Leaving his new wife of nine months our family home where Mum had loved us, brought us up . . . Anger and grief clashed. Sometimes I'd feel guilty for being so angry, or angry for feeling so sad.

School was over, my friends starting new education or careers. There was no structure or familiarity to my day. Despite the convent's expectations of me, I'd won a place at RADA. But now there was no way I could take it up. I couldn't afford to move to London and couldn't muster any type of creative energy to act. Besides, Lawrence, who was just sixteen, was deeply anxious and overwhelmed: I felt I couldn't leave him when really we were a unit, holding each other together. I needed him every bit as much

13

as he needed me. In the end, Auntie Sheila and Uncle Harry – not family, but friends of my mum and dad – took us in. I woke up each morning on the floor of their daughter's bedroom, desperate not to have to open my eyes. I had no goal, no parents, no guidance, no idea what to do. I felt like I was a boat bobbing on a vast grey sea of emptiness.

I hated the idea of people feeling sorry for me. In the Newton household, it wasn't the done thing to dwell on your misfortune. I was also embarrassed by the bizarreness of my situation. So I hid the pain and battled alone with thoughts of smashing my head through a glass window: anything to feel a pain different from the one raging through me.

The only solace came at weekends, when we'd pile into Tish's flat in London near where she was studying nursing. Being with my siblings again felt good – the squabbling, the teasing, the hierarchy that was never articulated but everyone understood. But whenever I'd try to talk to Tish about Mum and Dad, she'd shut down. Self-preservation was her survival technique. When things were too tough, she went in on herself. Her pain was too big, too raw to put into language. As kids, when Mum and Dad had been arguing, Tish would hole up in our bedroom. I'd be the one sitting, listening on the stairs, thinking that if I knew what was happening, I could help manage the outcome. I was the meerkat: always on the look-out, always on high alert.

Sometimes, I'd think I saw Mum in the street. I'd follow the redhead weaving through the crowds for a minute or so, allowing time for my brain to give in to the fantasy. But the loneliness

I felt when I let her go again was never worth it. I didn't realise at the time how exhausting constant vigilance would be. There was no therapy and no one dared ask how we were feeling. My friends tried to take me clubbing to distract me. They were embracing post-school freedom with big nights out. But you need to feel safe to let go and I couldn't lose control. I had to survive. When you have no one, you turn inwards. You have to generate your own self-belief. I couldn't have realised it then, but my resilience, my hardiness, would become a source of strength.

Shitty bedsits and second-hand creepers

IT WAS SEPTEMBER AND ALL the college places had been filled. But I knew that I needed structure. I found a college in Watford that still had a place available. The course was Visual Merchandising: learning how to dress shop windows. It didn't matter. I saw it as a stop-gap, nothing else.

With RADA gone, there was no clear path, no playbook. There weren't even parents to disappoint, though Tish soon assumed that role.

'What about becoming a paramedic?' she suggested one night, frustrated at my inertia. I didn't even bother answering back. I just went to bed, got up the next day, put my paint-splattered shirt back on and went to college again. What else could I do?

My colleagues were conscientious. I was angry and disruptive. 'You'll have no future in retail,' my course tutor was keen on telling me as she kept me late again to scrub a workbench I had spray-painted with the words 'Never Mind the Bollocks'.

'You've got to get a job when this course is over,' Tish reminded me. 'You can't keep being angry, Mary. How are you going to live? You can't keep staying at Aunty Sheila's, you must know that.'

I knew one of my course-mates had been offered a place at Harrods. I persuaded her to give me the number of her new boss and sneaked into the tutor's office in the studio one lunchtime to telephone him and try my luck. 'There's no more vacancies,' I was told, with short shrift by the display manager. But I didn't give up. I couldn't. Every day, over the next six weeks, I called. 'It's a personal matter,' I lied to get through the switchboard and to his line when they started screening my calls. Finally, he agreed to give me a chance.

So I headed to London to work as a window dresser at Harrods. The lure of landing a job at a hallowed department store was more impressive to my pals than it actually felt to me. I was a twenty-one-year-old kid, decked out in faded denim dungarees, virtually anonymous in a sea of professionals whose fingers seemed to conjure beauty out of thin air. I had to learn how to steam silk, how to pin without leaving marks, how to group product and props so they flowed and looked visually tempting. I'd also spend all day in their huge run of windows, hammering and staple-gunning fabric and props into place. It was physically exhausting. It became clear very quickly that it wasn't the perfection of styling that thrilled me. I wasn't a stylist. I had neither the interest nor the patience for it. It was the impact that great window concepts could make that got me excited. I didn't want to dress windows. I wanted to create them. But no junior would be trusted with that yet,

I lived in a shitty bedsit in Manor House, away from my family, with no one I knew, surrounded by money and luxury at work. Still, it felt good when I got my first pay packet: tearing off the perforated strips to reveal a number bigger than I'd ever seen before, although not one big enough to afford anything in the glossy halls of Harrods. I spent it on the £10 on-the-door returns for the latest play in Soho and second-hand creepers from Hyper Hyper, the Kensington Market stall that introduced me to some of the new ideas and names flooding London. They were patent, their shine reminding me of the optimism that started a new school year. I'd always loved the promise of a fresh start, of stripping the window displays out and starting again.

Back to life. Back to reality

WORK FILLED THE DAYS, BUT it was scary without the guy ropes of family and home – a lonely existence. Then I met Graham, a chemical engineer whose world couldn't have been more different to mine. It seemed every girl fancied Graham Portas. His dark thick curly hair, his deep brown eyes with lashes that any woman would have traded their last piece of chocolate for.

We dated casually for a few years. He'd moved to Wales to climb the corporate ladder in pharmaceuticals but would come back to London for Sunday roasts with his mum and nights out with me. 'Let's move in together,' he said one day. He was buying a house, putting down roots. Offering me a chance at a stability I hadn't known for years. I wanted that strength, the idea that someone would love and partner me.

Work gave me structure too. By now, I'd moved to Topshop – a retailer riding the wave of the British high street's boom. A new wave of professionals came in for polyester suits and commuter trainers. Twenty-somethings spent their first pay packet there on batwing sequin tops. As a window dresser, I was part of a team who helped draw them in. It was Graham who helped me realise it could be a profession, not just a pastime. 'You're clever, Mary,' he'd tell me. 'You should ask for more management training, apply for the next rung up.'

Graham had graduated with first-class honours in chemistry and maths, then moved seamlessly into a slick, corporate job. He helped me apply for a Display Manager job at Topshop – more responsibility, more money. It wasn't just his proof-reading of my job application that helped. It was his belief that I could do it. I had been lost for so many years. I'd had no sage, no guidance, no parents. Graham might have been unassuming himself, but he thrust me into the spotlight.

Suddenly, I had a team of four juniors, who looked to me for the vision. What were we trying to say with these windows? And how would we deliver it? My first job was to sell the Cyndi Lauper-style fluoro collections, so bright they made your eyes bleed. I trawled the art shops of Soho for rolls of orange and pink paper I then scrunched and folded to create a surreal sunset land-scape. I didn't need my boss to tell me it worked: the crowds that milled around the famous corner of Oxford Street told me I'd done something right. And so I followed that instinct, creating ever more elaborate displays.

My team were even younger than me, new to work and London. Their enthusiasm and energy was infectious.

The best stylist I had was Mandy. She was talented, but bloody crazy. I once pressed the button for Topshop's basement lift to take me to the shop floor. The doors opened to reveal Mandy in a handstand, fingers gripping the floor for dear life. Then, with a sudden yelp, she flopped forward and sprawled at my feet. Mandy once dressed a brilliant Buffalo window with mannequins in crop tops, dollar-sign necklaces, fake gold door-knocker earrings and trainers. She put a CD player in the corner of the window and played Neneh Cherry's 'Buffalo Stance' for the full three hours it took to finish the window. 'I've gotta feel it. And the music gives me the vibe,' she explained, sweating in her BodyMap shorts, vest and fingerless gloves. The collection sold out.

Everything we did seemed to just work. We persuaded Boy George to perform live in a window one Saturday, which stopped traffic – quite literally. One Christmas I covered the floor with thirty-two model penguins partnering mannequins dressed head to toe in black and white. It was inventive, fun and, most crucially, it was selling clothes.

The windows were attracting attention. And so was I. Before long, Topshop's chairman Sir Peter Stoneworth sought me out. He'd send a message down the chain, asking my boss's boss's boss to send me up to his office. I understood the eye-rolls from my colleagues. The rumours about so-called 'five times a night' Sir Peter were well-established albeit unproven. But I admired his charisma, his drive. The way he saw retail as show business, with him as the director.

He'd be at his desk by six each morning, making sure he was highly visible in the businesses he'd transformed – from a chain of department stores on every regional high street to Topshop, now an Oxford Street institution. He arrived in a chauffeur-driven Aston Martin each morning and wore his Rolex deliberately loose, so it was visible under his cuff – status symbols designed to show us what we were supposed to aspire to. Some thought it was gauche, but I understood his thirst. And my against-the-grain ideas suited his narrative that shopping could be entertainment.

In theory, I ticked all the boxes that said 'adult', but at work I'd still feel sick with stress as I gathered up my folder of ideas into my black plastic portfolio and headed to Sir Peter's office on the twelfth floor. It might have been the same building, but you could tell we were in the C-suite when the carpets changed from scrubby oatmeal to shag-pile magnolia.

It was at one of those meetings that he told me he wanted me to move to his newest acquisition, Harvey Nichols. A fusty department store whose clientele were, as far as I could tell, haughty South Kensington housewives didn't seem like a natural fit for me. I'd made Topshop windows a success by leaning into the youthful rebellion of the late 80s, attracting club kids and school kids who bought into the Madonna-soaked dream.

But you don't say no to Sir Peter. Just as you always feel you're in his debt.

Which is how I found myself watching London whizz by from the top deck of the 390 bus. Soul II Soul's *Club Classics Vol. One* is blaring out of my Walkman. 'Back To Life (However Do You Want Me)' has been number one for four weeks now. Much has been made of vocalist Caron Wheeler writing the song after she had a near-death experience before coming 'back to life' and finding her mission. It's practically impossible not to feel her joy – or to sing along.

We get to the corner of Knightsbridge and Sloane Square. I look down to see the red-brick façade of Harvey Nichols.

THE HERE AND NOW

Do women *really* live like this?

A s I APPROACH THE STAFF entrance I pause and hang back for a second. The metal shutters of the garage are open, a sleek black Mercedes parked up. Out of the front seat emerges first a black, patent six-inch stiletto, then a satin Wolford-stockinged leg and, finally, the full view of a waspishly thin woman. She scuttles into reception, me following behind clutching the windowed envelope that contains the letter from personnel offering me the job – proof that, even if I don't feel it, I do now belong here.

The receptionist is polite but cool. She asks me to wait while she phones for the assigned secretary who'll take me up to my office. I take a seat on the spongy brown sofa, the static making my skirt cling to my tights. I think about taking a newspaper to read, but they're lined up just so, stacked so that only the mast-heads are visible. They're so crisp, it's as if someone ironed them before laying them out.

'Good morning, Ms Portas, I'm Polly, but everyone calls me Bean,' says the perspiring young woman who bounds in to greet me. She explains she's nicknamed Bean because she resembled one as a baby. 'Wasn't a runner as you can see,' she adds self-mockingly. Her French Sole ballet shoes slip off the back of her feet as I follow her up the stairs, blisters still red on her heels.

Bean had got her job at Harvey Nichols via her aunt who was a high-flyer at Mishcon de Reya. Her aunt dropped her annual bonus on so much Nicole Farhi that when she asked the head of personal shopping if her niece could do an internship, Bean was in, and she'd never left.

She gives me the guided tour as we head to the fifth floor, offering up gossip eagerly. 'That's the fashion cupboard. They've just put a lock on the door though because there was a little incident last week when Martha was caught stealing the Alaïa samples,' she whispers. 'Don't use that bathroom – it's where Antonia goes to cry sometimes when she's having a tiff with her stepchildren,' comes next. She explains that the woman I'd seen getting out of the car that morning was Antonia Allard, the store's Fashion Director, in charge of deciding which designers get stocked on the shop floor. It makes sense then that she was wearing the most perfect Thierry Mugler coat. Double-fronted cashmere, belted tightly to show off her waist.

'Oh, and it's Antonia,' she cautions. 'Never Toni.' As we near my office, she shyly introduces me to Mr and Mrs Anstey, the husband-and-wife duo who manage the in-house restaurant, Harvey's at the Top. Peering past them, I see waiters in black tie serving crystal glasses of sherry to a group of women sitting bolt upright on the leather banquettes. I glance at my watch: it's 10.30 a.m. on a Monday.

Finally, we reach my office. The man I've taken over from left to start his role as Head of Visuals at the V&A weeks ago, but, walking in, it's like he's still in situ. Solid mahogany bookshelves are lined with dusty tomes on Tuscan columns and Sir John Soane's works. There's a record player with the complete symphonies of Beethoven lined up neatly beside them. Dark green walls and oriental rugs suck up the light; it's more a drawing room than an office. Bean's left a carafe of water and a single glass on the desk. As I sit down and pull the chain on the brass banker's lamp, I wonder what I'm actually supposed to do first.

I'm sorting through my portfolio of cuttings – postcards I've collected from galleries over the years, pages ripped out of *Vogue* – when my boss Callum raps on my door. 'She's arrived,' he laughs, mock-bowing. 'Welcome, Ms Portas. Shall we take a walk?' I leave my suit jacket hanging on the Edwardian coat stand in the corner, the orange looking faintly ridiculous against the stained oak.

Sales Director Callum Baird had risen through the ranks: Edinburgh University, then Unilever, then British Airways and their Club World, and finally to here. Along the way, he'd lost his Scottish accent but gained a wit that instantly put me at ease. 'Here we have accounts, legal, personnel and the women who everyone smart knows are really in charge: the personal assistants,' he says smoothly as he shows me around. 'Before I hire anyone, I ask them that mighty question: what do you like about luxury?

The ones who come in have said something believable in answer to that question. So they're all at the very least dynamic.'

'I remember,' I laugh.

I'd talked about my mother when answering Callum's interview question. She had so little money for luxuries, I was always fascinated by what she chose to spend it on. Often it was soaps and body creams – her potions, she used to jokingly call them. It wasn't about the label or the bottle – though they were often quite beautiful too. It was about the way she felt applying that rose-scented body cream each night at her dressing table. The rare act of doing something just for herself.

'My answer must have done its job, I guess,' I say now as we head into Callum's office.

'Oh yes,' Callum replies. 'You're going to fit in well here, Mary. I can tell.'

As Sales Director, his primary objective is hitting the weekly sales targets – numbers that are reported each Tuesday in the board meeting. I'm there to help him achieve that by creating innovative ways to draw customers into the store – starting with window displays. 'And the more successful you are, Mary, the better I'll look,' he says, half in jest, half warning. We both know this job is a big step up for me. Where my youth and radical ideas might have served me well at Topshop, here they could well be my downfall.

He explains that the core Harvey Nichols shopper is English and from old money. Most live within five miles of the store – not that you'd know it from the drivers who parked up on

Lowndes Square ready to take their shopping bags home and their charges to lunch at Daphne's. Plummy mummy-and-daughter duos wander the shop floor together – all pleated skirts, strands of pearls and puffy velvet hairbands. They're not looking for anything in particular, more killing time until the weekend.

I soon discover women like this don't just shop at Harvey Nichols – they work here too. There's a Sloane in the press office who everyone calls Lady Scratch Arsehole. 'You can't host a launch window event on a Thursday. Everybody goes to the country then,' she trills at me in her high-pitched, nasal voice. The publicity team resent that she's been brought in by the MD, a favour for a friend-of-a-long-lost-friend despite the fact that she'll only work four days a week. 'I'm utterly fatigued by the time Thursday comes around,' she sighs every week as she unties her 'Knightsbridge knotted' scarf from her handbag to put around her head. Still, no one can deny she makes up for trotting off to the countryside every Friday by hosting successful afternoon shopping tea parties for her contacts. She invites all her chums, the poshos who have lots of dosh but few ways to fill their days, to previews of new stock. Over cucumber sandwiches, the shop-floor managers whisk in rails of ball gowns and Barbours for them to fight over before everyone retires for a well-stewed pot of Earl Grey. The hand-knitted tea cosies she uses are shaped like crowns. Which makes sense because Harvey's most famous customer is Princess Diana.

I'm told that it is Antonella Filbert, Head of Private Client Relations, who coordinates visits by royalty, Hollywood or similar. A voice like butter, she's warm but steely. We call her the velvet hammer. Antonella is in her forties, and single – or so we guess as we know so little about her. She's as discreet with us as she is with the private clients she styles. We don't really know if she has a partner or where her family comes from. But we can make a good guess that it's money – old or new – because she lives in a beautiful apartment just behind Harrods. I saw her one day clutching a bag of groceries from the food hall there. Word has it that she hosts intimate soirées, effortlessly pulling together her network of high-profile and very high-net-worth individuals. She has a constant fixed smile that's a multi-purpose survival tool, perfected for superstars and royal aides. You wouldn't know if she was thinking 'that's a terrific idea' or 'please get out my private client suite, you total and utter fuckwit'. There are layers of quiet mystery that surround her. I find her utterly fascinating.

Antonella is impeccably professional and tactful about Lady Diana's visits, but you know when the princess is in the store. There'll be a sudden drop in the temperature of the noise, like just before a curtain comes up on a show. And you'll see Antonella come out of her office to swat away staff hovering outside, desperate to catch a glimpse of the woman who's given the Royal Family sex appeal. 'Shooo, shooo, shooo,' she scoffs.

You've got to start somewhere

I HAVE A TEAM OF eighteen working with me, a mixture of experts in carpentry, prop-making, signage and those who can drape, pin and style clothes in such a way as to make the customer stop, stare – and shop. They're all based in the studio on the top floor of the store. As I enter the sawdust-strewn space, I get the sense that some of them aren't keen on having a new boss. Or, rather, me as their new boss.

There's Ruth, whose speciality is beautiful paint effects. She can turn a piece of MDF into a sunset with just a few strokes. A lovely buxom Jewish girl, her uniform is a low-cut black body, DMs and an unbuttoned plaid shirt covered in paint no matter how many times she washes it.

Jules is the one the team turn to for signage. Her calligraphy is as precise and pretty as her hair, coiffed in Madonna-esque platinum curls. I watch her handwrite with brush and ink on a placard: *New designer: Adrienne Vittadini, Floor 3.* We'll use this to try and direct people to the woman who's become known as 'The Queen of Knits' in Hollywood. We're stocking her exclusively.

Junior stylist Cass is my nightclub girl – I soon learnt never to ask her on a Monday morning what she'd been up to at the weekend. It would usually end with a story of a mash-up at Turnmills or the Astoria, sometimes a field rave. When Cass isn't asleep under a workbench, she works with a ferocious energy pumping out Pearl Jam, occasionally wearing a Vivienne Westwood crown. Because, why not?

Sam runs carpentry. The team call him Jesus on account of his beard, long hair and, obviously, his profession. He doesn't say a word. But he knows his way around a lathe.

Meanwhile, it's hard to get a word in edgeways with the two senior stylists Des and Donald – The Double Ds, as I'd come to call them. Des is a bear of a man with a huge beard, battered Levi's and razor-sharp sarcasm. I had known of his work before when I was at Topshop and he was at Miss Selfridge. 'She was more Bananarama, not high fashion then, boys. Hair all dodgy tips and streaks,' I catch him telling the team when he thinks I'm out of earshot. Donald's been at Harvey Nichols for years. He comes from old money, had studied at the Courtauld and is now in his mid-forties, all of which means he's unusual in a visual team that are otherwise all in their twenties.

'Well, that's not the way we've typically done it,' I hear from Donald time and time again as I try to talk to my team about new ideas over the coming weeks. It's clear the challenge will be how to bring in fresh ideas and a new customer base without alienating not only the old classic customers but also my own team.

Bringing them together is the answer, I decide. Weekly brain-storms, where we'll spend a fast and furious hour riffing over ideas and getting to know each other better. I've always believed that personal connection is crucial in any successful team. I ask Bean to schedule them for 10 a.m. each Tuesday. That way we'll have been able to analyse the weekend trading numbers and spend Monday checking off our to-do lists before we add new ideas to them.

I tell everyone to come with ideas – they're the lifeblood of any creative industry. I want to know what they've seen, what's inspired them, what made them stop, laugh or gasp.

'Jules, what did you do this weekend?' I ask to kick things off.

'I went to the British Museum actually. All that chat about the Elgin Marbles made me think I'd better see them while I still can,' she replies, looking up at me for approval. It's not hard to tell Jules is a perfectionist, but it'll get in her way. She'll say the thing she thinks you want to hear, not what she's actually thinking.

I'm not interested in hifalutin art and culture: I want realness from this team.

'I don't think you need to stress, Jules. They're not going anywhere fast. Too much of a political hot potato that one,' I say, turning to Cass. 'What about you?'

Cass bites into half a Rolo, a string of caramel sliding down her chin. She's drama, this girl.

'I went to Nanny Seaside's,' she starts, chomping down the chocolate. 'She's mad, my nan, a proper hoarder. She's got this flat in Lee-on-Solent, third floor, windows overlooking the beach. What's funny is that she's lined up her porcelain dolls in the window, their creepy little glass eyes all staring right over the shingle. Poor buggers. It's like she's dressed the windows not for her but for anyone walking past. It'll give 'em quite the fright.'

'Let's riff off that,' I interject. 'It could be brilliant. What could you have dolls like that showing off?'

'Not clothes, I can tell you that for free,' Cass replies. 'All frilly bonnets and crispy hair.'

'It'd be good for the shoe display,' pipes up Des. 'You could play with that. Velvet frock coats and ruffled collars but with those punchy neon platforms that are everywhere.'

'We could get Jesus to build them some cases so it looks like they're brand-new dolls, all boxed up ready for some kid to buy,' adds Donald. The room's got energy now. I love watching an idea flourish, each person adding petals until it's fully in bloom.

'The accessories windows are too narrow and high. The shape won't work,' Ruth butts in, the first thing she's said all brainstorm.

'Give it a rest, Ruth,' shoots back Cass. 'Just because you can't see a way to get your paint into it, don't mean you have to trash it.'

There's always one, I think. That person who sucks the oxygen out of the room. The only way to deal with vampires like her is to kill them with sunlight.

'Well, I love a sharp, subversive twist on the traditional.' I smile. 'It's just what we should be doing here.'

Sadly, MD Ken Hagen's more in Ruth's camp when the windows debut. 'It looks like you've stuck Chucky in there,' he barks.

It's true the glassy-eyed dolls staring out onto Sloane Street are creepier than I'd intended. But you can't deny that makes you look at them twice, drawn to the camp twist on something macabre. You can't quite work out what to think about the windows and that's what I like about them.

As 10 a.m. Tuesdays become a team ritual, Rolos and all, the ideas start to flow more freely. Donald brings in an article about the new work from graphic designer Barbara Kruger – a picture of a black-and-white hand holding a credit card, overlaid with type saying 'I Shop Therefore I Am'. 'Saw this when she did an exhibition at the Serpentine. It's an indictment of how women are particularly targeted by the consumer culture. She's also saying that most people are no longer defined by what they think but by what they own. The original was obviously Descartes – I think therefore I am. I think this is really clever and reckon she's right.'

We sit in silence.

'I think she's right too, Donald. But saying it in our windows while displaying a £500 bag feels a bit shit, don't you think?'

We swiftly move on and decide that since the whole world seems to have fallen for rom-com *When Harry Met Sally* a cutesy knitwear window won't harm. It feels lighter, easier. But something stays with me – quiet and unsettled. I haven't worked out what it is yet, but it's there, waiting for its moment.

It's not quite seamless yet, though. Des and I can't make sense of the meeting notes Bean transcribed for us.

'*Playboy?*' Des asks, confused. 'I don't remember you signing off on a *Playboy* window, Mary.'

'Hmm, me neither,' I reply. 'Bean! Can I borrow you for a minute?'

'What does this mean?' I ask my sweet but hopeless secretary.

'Oops-a-daisy,' Bean exclaims. 'I think I meant Game Boy. It was when you were talking about whether we should put tech on display.'

'Not getting enough, eh, love?' Des teases as Bean blushes as red as a kidney bean.

Rivals

WHEN YOU ALREADY FEEL LIKE an imposter, it's easy to let others treat you that way. Especially in a place where age-old subtle signals and social codes of class still pervade. Antonia Allard certainly didn't need much encouragement to posh it up and show hers off.

Antonia Allard had style. Just the right side of louche silk shirts. Cigarette pants. Layers of bangles stacked up her arm, massive rings and a crucifix pendant. She reminded me of Charles Bukowski's poem, 'style'. 'style is the answer to everything – / a fresh way to approach a dull or a / dangerous thing. / to do a dull thing with style / is preferable to doing a dangerous thing without it.'

Admittedly it helped that, as Fashion Director, Antonia held the purse strings. Which is why her office was always full of beautiful samples, dustbags and suit carriers discarded as she unwrapped gift after gift. There weren't enough vases for the flowers sent from designers to curry favour. Cream, waxy camellias were her favourite. 'You can't better Coco,' she'd say, of the Chanel founder, who was famously sent bouquets of camellias by her lover. I wondered if it was less the romance that appealed; rather the notion that the flower – which blooms in winter yet never loses its leaves – is the ultimate symbol of resilience. A survivor.

Antonia had spent her late teens and early twenties working in Paris, after leaving the Lycée François in London early. 'Fabulous now, neglectful then,' she once told me about her schooling. Her godmother worked in the lingerie world alongside the woman who designed underwear for Princess Margaret and had taken Antonia under her wing. 'Because of her, I ended up renting my first apartment from the sister of the wife of the now Chairman at Louis Vuitton,' she rattled off when she took me out to lunch at Joe's café on Sloane Street, an occasion which felt more about establishing herself than welcoming me. 'He gave me a job. And from there, Dior, Le Bon Marché, Londres, and, finalement, ici, Harvey's.'

She took her job as seriously as maintaining her twenty-three-inch waist. She'd spent years curating clever collections that kept the Gussie & Co. customers happy but also reflected the speed, energy and sex appeal of the 80s. The biggest proportion of spend went on quiet luxury. Brands like Jean Muir, Nicole Farhi, Jasper Conran, who could be relied on for a classic cashmere coat, exquisitely cut trousers or a dress that wouldn't scare the husband or the housekeeper.

Many of the brands we stocked were thanks to Antonia's relationships with Britain's leading designers. Joseph Ettedgui, known simply as Joseph, was her favourite. He had an achingly cool emporium down the road designed by the architect of the moment, Eva Jiřičná. Joseph was one of the first to put a restaurant into a fashion shop, and Antonia loved popping into Joe's for a salad and a fag. Often Joseph himself would come and sit with us, cigar in hand. 'Bonjour, mesdames,' he'd say, his French–Moroccan accent as strong as when he moved to London in the 60s. 'What do you think of my walls? Black, c'est bon, n'est-ce pas? Some think it's too much black. But the only way you can make a colour beautiful is by spending a lot of money.'

'Joseph is so clever,' she whispers. 'Fashion and food go so well together. Although if one likes fashion, one can't like food too much,' she sniffs as I order a club sandwich. 'It inhibits the ability to fit into the clothes, as we know all too well.'

Antonia is proud that women are coming into Harvey Nichols to seek out the personality pin-stripe trousers and waistcoats from Joseph's latest collection. 'I know talent, and it knows me,' she reminds me.

Colour and statement pieces are also flying amongst a new, emerging customer base: women with their own pay packets and the confidence to pull off clothes that'll help them stand out. We can't keep Claude Montana big-shouldered suits in stock, even though the price is enough to feed a household of four for a month. I still can't get my head round this kind of wealth.

Meanwhile, the British duo Keith Varty and Alan Cleaver, who took over from Gianni Versace at the Italian fashion label Byblos, are hot property. Their jackets are sleek, bold and playfully flamboyant, just like them. I find myself increasingly drawn to their style, but Antonia is less sure. As much as she adores their style, she sometimes finds their outlandishness errs on the side of insolence. 'I've tried to warn them that today's peacocks are tomorrow's feather duster,' she sighs.

I soon learn that eveningwear is also big business, something Antonia has successfully petitioned to have bespoke fittings for. Each brand has been given a partitioned rectangular space around the perimeter of the womenswear floor, their names printed in black letters on the crisp, white back wall. Bruce Oldfield, Jacques Azagury, Bellville Sassoon: all the names the Harvey Nichols women love are represented. Antonia is in the process of negotiating an exclusive collection of Frank Usher little black dresses, with the lower price points she hopes will bring in a younger crowd ahead of Christmas. It's clear she's got substance, not just style.

Antonia's astute enough about the business to instinctively understand the allure of newness, but she's used to being the person who brings it into Harvey Nichols. When I'm riffing off the idea of Jeff Koons-style high-gloss mirrors and balloons for a new window display, she allows herself the rarity of a frown. 'Mais non. You haven't even seen the Cruise collections I've bought, n'est-ce pas vrai,' she'd say, her habit of slipping in French affectations as confusing as the cadence of the luxury fashion calendar. She wants windows built around the clothes she's bought for the shop floor, not abstract ideas from upstarts dressed in old Topshop samples.

She's making a habit of dropping sample gifts on my desk. 'Thought you could do with this. Jasper's shirts are worth their weight in silk,' she writes on the note. She doesn't need to sign it, I'd recognise her spidery handwriting anywhere. When the summer sales start, she suggests we go to the staff preview together. Then curates my rail: all basics, all black. The Joseph trousers she pulls out for me are too small, even though I'm a size 10. With a thin smile and a raised brow, she says, 'Well, that was ambitious of me. Let me see what I've got from designers who cut on the more generous side.'

The golden goose

ANTONIA MIGHT HAVE GOT ME looking the part, but I'm worried the windows still aren't quite connecting with the MD or the audience. And I've got to present my Christmas plans next week.

In retail, Christmas is the most important time of the year. For well over half the sector, Christmas accounts for quarter of their annual revenue. It's the golden goose – you can't afford to over-cook it.

Bean has created a planogram for me, showing the schemes and fittings schedules for the windows throughout the year. January Sales, First Spring (debuting spring/summer collections), Second Spring and so on . . . She might be hopeless at shorthand, organ-ising meetings, getting to work on time and generally being efficient at anything, but she's taken this to heart, colour-coding the A3 sheet in such detail I have to keep consulting the key. There is one box you can't miss, though: Christmas in July. We usually work at least three months ahead, but for Christmas, where the stakes are so high, planning starts in the summer. Pinned on a board opposite my desk, circled in yellow highlighter, I've been staring at it for weeks.

I already have a vague inkling of what our competitors will do. Harrods, like their egomaniacal, tasteless owner, will be throwing more money than style at their Christmas windows. I laugh as I imagine artificial icicles encrusted with Swarovski crystals hanging above trees wrapped in strings of pearls, every detail screaming excess. I spare a thought for their poor display manager trying to get any sophisticated ideas through to that chairman. Liberty, unlike Harrods, oozes class: majoring in nostalgic, artistic story-telling, beautifully curated. They'll probably go for a mix of nature and fantasy. Selfridges will have Santa in his grotto, mechanised elves tapping away with their hammers – they do the same thing every year. I want ours to feel different. If I've learnt anything so far, it's this: you know deep down inside when an idea feels right. I haven't worked out how to explain that when I present to the board, but I feel it like an electric current running through me. On the one hand I feel buzzy with energy and excitement; on the other an odd calmness. A voice inside me, says with utter conviction, *This Is It.*

That's the feeling I've explained to the team as we get together in my office to brainstorm Christmas on what ends up being the hottest day of the year so far. Ever the joker, Des minces in with his beard spray-painted white for the occasion. 'Ho-ho-ho,' he laughs until the studio gets so warm with everyone in it his beard starts dripping all over his black vest. The team throws out suggestions to get the ball rolling. I dismiss a Garden of Eden scheme, Kew Gardens-style. That might attract the wrong sort of attention. Candy canes, with mannequins dressed in red and white, feels too twee. Let's leave that to Selfridges.

'I'm thinking punk royalty. Everyone's obsessed with Charles and Di, aren't they?' pipes up Cass. 'We could make it, like, a really posh English house, butler and all, holding a silver tray. But the mannequins are killing it. It's all a bit of a fucked-up tartan suit. A load of Mohawk wigs.' She's on her feet now. 'You could have a family sitting down around a telly. And, yeah, you'd have the Queen, like, on the telly. She's doing her speech. The family watching, they'd be wearing them shitty Frank Usher dresses. That'd keep Antonia quiet. But then there's signage saying "God Save the Couture" in the background. Maybe with letters cut out of old *Hello!* mags.' She even wants the Sex Pistols tune blaring out of speakers onto the street.

'Oh, give it a rest, Cass,' Des sighs. 'As if Antonia and Ken would ever go for that.'

'Des,' I interject quickly, 'it's a brainstorm. And in a brainstorm, everyone has a voice.'

Mind you, he's not wrong. I worry it's too rebellious. And we couldn't risk losing the Royal Warrant, what with all the cash it brings in from travelling Yanks.

'So, Des, have you got anything?' I throw out to him. 'What's everyone wearing in the gay bars at the moment?'

'It's all Grace Jones still when it comes to Christmas at the clubs, Mary. So you could go sci-fi, metallic bodysuits . . . But I reckon it's more ripped mesh tops, studded harnesses with spiked vests and some fucking hot pink fishnet stockings for the old birds of Knightsbridge to slip into on Christmas Eve,' he snaps back, not much use. Des can be my biggest asset, but he can also be a pain in the arse when he's in one of his fuck-the-establishment, knife-edge moods.

I settle on Baroque. But Baroque with sex appeal. I know the board will accept a classic option, but at least I can make it opulent. I've been obsessing over Peter Greenaway's latest film, *The Cook, the Thief, His Wife & Her Lover*. I'd heard Greenaway arguing in an interview that the Old Testament got it wrong. In the beginning was not the Word, he proclaimed. In the beginning was the Image. I fell in love with his crazy, opulent, theatrical, symbolic tableaus. His cinema shots displayed like paintings in a frame. It's a perfect parallel, I feel. My windows are the frames; what's inside them, the painting.

I excitedly start a visual mood board, tearing through V&A catalogues and old copies of *The World of Interiors* to start building a picture of what's in my head. Pompidou-style wigs, scrolls, gilt frescoes on the domed ceilings, frilled collars and cuffs, the rich reds and burnt oranges you see in the costumes of Old Masters hanging in the National Gallery. I add Raphael's *Triumph of Galatae* painting. It was the reference point of a collection by Dolce & Gabbana, a new Italian duo whose show was the talk of Milan Fashion Week. Technically, it's Renaissance, but the cherubs are cute. Anyway, Peter Greenaway didn't give a crap about realism so neither will I.

'I'd say that's more Rococo,' Antonia muses when I show her what I'm thinking. Her tone is casual, but it sends me spiralling:

a reminder that my love of everything from Shakespeare's sonnets to stories of Studio 54 can never compete with the self-assurance of someone educated at the Lycée.

I'm beginning to understand how this place works, unpicking the politics of the relationship between Antonia and Callum. They might technically be on the same level, paid a similar wage, but the reality is more complicated.

To the outside world, the real kudos sits with Antonia's role. In a world where so many luxury brands desperately need department stores to reach a wider audience than their singular, smaller boutiques, she's the power-broker. Even more so for brands without their own store all together. There's a reason the story of Ralph Lauren starting out selling ties to New York Fifth Avenue department store Saks has become so legendary. And why designers are so obsequious around Antonia. What her team decide to buy from their stock can make or break their brand – and Harvey Nichols itself.

Underneath Antonia is a team that works across all the categories we stock. They're all women in their thirties up, who hang out of the window smoking and have MTV running constantly on the JVC TV that sits in the corner of their office. The antenna still has a sprig of tinsel on it from last year's office party. Jess does knitwear, Mils swimwear and lingerie, Suze accessories and hosiery, and Bella heads up new designers. She's my favourite.

★

Bella travels constantly, her life a rollercoaster of bringing in newness without destroying the department's chances of hitting their exacting sell-through target by having enough of the core categories that'll satisfy the traditional Harvey Nichols customer. The team are judged on how much of the product they buy sells profitably. Antonia and co. need to take risks, but they can't afford for them not to pay off.

Once the stock chosen by Antonia's team hits the Harvey Nichols loading bay though, the responsibility for shifting it falls to Callum. Sales directors are there to run the store, making sure every inch of the floorplan, every decision is optimised for profit. It's a role heavy on logistics, operations and analysis: getting deliveries onto the shop floor, working out where they should be positioned, tracking if product is selling and, if not, why not. Callum is in constant dialogue with the shop-floor managers and pores over their daily sell-through reports. He'll use these to work out how quickly to move stock off the floor or when we'll move into sale – opting to take a hit on margins but shift product. He's also in charge of concessions. These are essentially brand shops within Harvey Nichols who pay a percentage to be in the store. Callum loves these as they are an easy way to hit targets with their guaranteed revenue. Antonia doesn't. She thinks they bring down the brand image and she would far rather have that space for what she's chosen to buy.

There's always tension between Callum and Antonia. It's easier to blame each other if they don't meet their profit margins. The buy wasn't right, Callum will say. They went into sale prematurely, Antonia will shoot back. She'll also be concerned that brands she's spent years nurturing to give her exclusives won't like seeing their product cheapened by a 30% off swing tag.

In many ways, my team and I feel more of an affinity to Antonia's way of thinking. Graduates of design, art and fashion colleges, my team of rowdy anarchists see what they do as creating art, beauty, storytelling through clothes. But I report into Callum.

Callum has more nuance and insight than the typical sales directors I've met in previous retail businesses. But, like most, he sees visual merchandising as a sales job: there to shift product. Which is why I'm determined to happily position my role between the two: making sure I have a solid grasp of the numbers while pushing creative boundaries. I love nothing better than seeing the commercial impact of my instinctive ideas and concepts delivering tangible business results. It's proof to me that creativity is a powerful business force. And I know it's the way to win over Ken Hagen. He really only cares about cash – not how it comes in.

I suppose you don't get to be managing director of a retail giant without being driven and smart, but Ken has the playbook nailed. Small, American, always impeccably dressed, he's got that unmistakable 80s Wall Street look – sharp Brooks Brothers suits, the kind that say old money but with just enough flash to hint at ambition.

He's picked up a penchant for Etro after his transfer to Europe to run Harvey Nichols, and he especially loves educating the other men with his knowledge. 'Those Italians know how to make a suit. They are effortless,' he says. 'A whisper of structure instead of a shout, a glide instead of a march, unlike the British ones; they're too structured and buttoned-up, just like y'all.'

Callum has given me some tips about how to present a crisp

deck for Ken. 'You get two and a half minutes before he'll want to have his own say,' he warns. So I'm holding only one thing as I walk to his office: a supersize version of my mood board, which I've had Bean blow up onto 10mm foam.

As I talk him through it, he leans back in his chair, lights a Pall Mall and puts feet up on his desk. His office stinks of stale fags and Creed Bois du Portugal. 'Looks a bit dark to me,' he interjects after ninety seconds. 'But fine. Just make sure you can see the bloody clothes.' It's like he feels he has to say something, even if it means nothing.

But I don't care. The Christmas countdown is on.

The Double Ds

THE NEXT MORNING, I HEAD to the studio to brief the boys. Now we'll have to sketch the look and feel of each window, then do the technical drawings and finally the 3D images that'll ensure they're architecturally sound. Long and narrow, the windows on Seville Street are the toughest to design. Window 12, the curved showstopper that looks out onto Sloane Street, the most crucial. It's the shop window to Harvey Nichols, quite literally. 'Better put the most expensive dress in there, Mary,' Callum would say, classic salesman.

No one from my team will be around yet. The first thing the team is supposed to do is what's called a floor check, where they head to the floor they've been assigned and check the windows and cases. They'll dust the mannequin bases, remove any dead flies – the lighting loves to frazzle a bluebottle – and check nothing's fallen over, no item knocked out of place. But a rare half an hour in the studio by myself is precious. The smell of acrylics reminds

52

me of my days as a junior in the window displays at Harrods when my job was simply to create, not dictate.

Walking in though, I see Des draped in a piece of purple brocade while Cass is standing over him, fabric scissors in hand. He's having his hair cut.

'Pass me this month's *Face*,' he asks a junior. 'I'm just having a little trim,' he laughs.

This is the sort of management situation I dread. The easiest thing to do would be to ignore it, to walk away. I know Des thinks he's just pissing about, playing up to the crowd, so is it really worth me telling him off? Can I be bothered with the fallout of a confrontation with him and his laser-sharp comebacks? I'll need to steel myself. But, in my heart, I also know I can't unsee this. That behind Des's comedy act is a sense that he can skirt the bits of the job he finds boring and thinks are beneath him. Besides, Des is at risk of infecting Cass with that attitude too. And once that seeps through the team, it's a bloody nightmare to manage. Des's contrariness makes him a brilliant, live-wire creative, but I need him to use it to deliver, not disrupt. Because, and here's what makes him so frustrating, when he's at his best, he really is one of the best I've worked with.

'This isn't going to be an easy conversation, but it's one we have to have,' I tell Des the next morning. I've asked to see him first thing, preferring to get anything disciplinary out the way before the day kicks in. Partly, it means I can't put it off, but also I never think it's good to send a staff member home stewing for the evening.

'Your work is exceptional, but your behaviour is anything but,' I chastise him. 'If we want the board to leave us alone so we can do our best work, they have to trust us. You pissing about doesn't help. You can't pick and choose the bits of the job you want to do.'

Des nods, but his natural defensiveness means he won't give in that easily. 'Come on, Mary. I get it, but the floor check's a waste of our time. We could be doing something so much more creative than cleaning. And dusting the displays in menswear is hell. I'm surrounded by beautiful sharply dressed blokes while I'm over by the mannequins battling away with self-esteem and a bleeding feather duster.'

'Des, you know as well as I do that keeping the displays dusted and in order is a fundamental part of the job. It takes thirty minutes each day and is done,' I reply. 'I expect you all to have enough professional pride that you want your work to stand out for the right reasons. But if you think there's a better way of organising the team's workload, I'm open for ideas.'

I pause, waiting. But nothing comes back. 'And send someone else to the men's floor. Someone straight who doesn't fancy any of them. That's an easy fix.'

'OK, OK,' Des replies, holding up his hands. 'I'll have a think.'

I think he's finally understood my impatience isn't waning – and that he needs to get me back on side. 'Besides, you've got to understand the team look up to you. I need you to set them an example. Cass is talented, but she's impressionable. You know that . . .' I sigh. 'Now let's move on,' I finish. I've said my piece, made my point. I've tried to be clear and concise so there's no room for interpretation. But I also think it's important that, once it's said, we don't let it fester. That won't help me, or the team dynamics.

Overall, I do think the team is well-balanced: some are brilliant at props and painting, others at grouping the window space powerfully and beautifully. Then there are the ones who can curate the clothes so they inspire and delight any onlooker. On a good day, Des's got it all: bold, sharp ideas to shape the vision of a window and the physicality to fit displays so they're rock solid – and safe. An expert carpenter, we sometimes joke the only reason Des keeps his beard so bushy is so that he always has ready access to the pencil he keeps poking out of it.

It's why, off-the-book haircuts aside, Des will always be my first choice to work on the front windows. When he's paired with Donald, it's fascinating to watch. Precise and thoughtful, no one can mould wire quite like Donald. It sounds simple, but manipulating wire is one of the most crucial skills for a window dresser. It requires a steady hand and an imaginative mind to create shapes that clothes can hang from. Donald can drape a scarf so it looks like angel wings. 'Dressing something is a dance. You move. It lands. It's obviously got to be alive,' Donald had once told me, when I asked him why he'd been doing the same job for years without once going for a promotion.

Over the coming months, the Double Ds work together to bring a slice of Baroque to Knightsbridge. Milky-white cherubs are painted onto planks of wood with a precision Michelangelo would approve of. Props are made, plaster of Paris painstakingly poured into decorative moulds that will make up the architraves. I'm up and down from my office to the studio, unfurling swathes of fabric as we search for the right shades of velvet. Nirvana's album *Bleach* blasts out while they work. It's Christmas c/o Kurt Cobain.

The team is petitioning me for new mannequins, but we can't afford them. As the year has bled away, so has the budget. 'You'll just have to send the ones that work for a respray,' I tell a grumpy Donald.

He's been up in the eaves all morning, where the bodies (mannequins) are buried (stored), finding the ones with poses he thinks he can make look dramatic and dynamic. One has a hand in a semi-circle in the air, almost ballet fourth position, as if mid grand gesticulation. Another, hands-on-hips and leg thrust forward to show off some thigh.

By the time the windows are ready to fit, the studio looks like we've just looted the Palace of Versailles. But before we can install Baroque Christmas, the old window displays must be stripped and the detritus hauled to the skips in the loading bay. Then, the team must rebuild from the floor upwards. It's a tough job, but worse in the winter when the MDF floor slabs that are laid as a foundation are cold and brittle. I watch as Des and Donald, along with Cass and Jesus, the carpenter, use hair dryers to soften the PVC plastic, bending and stretching it so it will be pliable enough to cover the huge floor panels. They're sweating despite wearing next to nothing.

When the floor is ready, the Double Ds lug down the manne-quins. One arm around the mannequin's neck, the other its crotch, even Donald can't make this look elegant. As he barges through the perfumery department, sweating and swearing, the assistants on the shop floor mutter their disdain to each other. Before he's even finished sidling the mannequin behind their counters to access the window, they've started spraying Guerlain's L'Heure Bleue frantically into the air. The Queen's favourite fragrance cures all.

Meanwhile, behind blinds that read 'Pardon our appearance whilst we refit our windows' Des and Donald get to work. They unspool wire coated with cotton, then wrap a couple of lengths around the waist of the mannequins, one pulled down to the ground between her legs, the other sitting just slightly forward. Bang a nail just a touch into the PVC, twist the wire around tight and then a final hammer right into the ground. 'Hear that?' says Des, twanging the wire like a piano string. 'She's not going anywhere.'

Confident the mannequins won't be crashing through the front window any time soon, the boys haul huge sacks of glitter into the display. When they upend them to pour it across the floor, plumes of glitter fill the air. 'It's camper than a night in Heaven in here!' squeals Donald, kicking a mound up against Des.

They start to move the props into place. This is a dance, where precision and placement are key. 'Time for lights,' Des shouts as Cass scarpers up the ladder to the floodlights that'll give the mannequins a halo effect. 'Left a bit. Try tilting it forward a touch,' Donald instructs Cass, from the street. 'Ready for curtains up.'

Antonia might think the windows start with the clothes, that they're the most crucial element, but for me they're secondary to the scene. I know the windows are there to sell clothes, but I've always believed that the first step in creating a successful window is the idea, the visual concept.

It's like starting a conversation between the shop and the people who walk by. I want to grab their attention. Turn their heads. Make an unforgettable impression. I want my windows to surprise people. To stop them in their tracks, get them out of their busy heads and make them feel like they're stepping into another story, another life, one more beautiful, more fabulous than their own. My windows should offer an escape from the drudge of their daily reality. But, more than that, I want people to stop, stare and feel something. It might be 'that's bonkers' or 'that's beautiful' or 'that's just bloody wonderful', but it should always end with: 'I want to be part of that.' That's what'll make customers come to the shop floor.

Or so I think.

'This is the collection we really need you to get behind this season,' the floor managers say, ushering us towards the rails of Ben de Lisi dresses. 'We're stocking it exclusively, so we need it to sell. Prominent space in the windows would help.' But we don't want plum and peach chiffon dresses, we want Galliano and Gucci. We're looking for knockout gowns and bobby-dazzler diamonds. Each piece we request must be signed out in the Stock Movement book, a tome that weighs more than a Baroque bible. And is almost as significant. As Donald fills out a chit, recording the Gucci suit he wants for window 12, floor managers surround him in a flap. 'You can't have that one. We need it for the shop floor,' they cry in unison.

Donald's done this before. The number of times we have explained to the sales team the rationale behind how we choose the window pieces is enough to make us qualify for sainthood. 'It's a very simple strategy,' he explains patiently. In essence, putting the showstopper pieces in the window draws people in by showing them excitement – a sense of wonder and possibility. We want to make them think, 'Ooh, that's amazing! Can I really get away with wearing that?' Once inside, they'll more often than not realise they can't and choose the simpler, safer options, but it's the excitement of the bold display that pulled them through in the first place.

Before the windows can officially open to the public, I have to show Ken. At this stage, there's not much he can actually do if he hates the displays, but in a place where hierarchy rules, it helps cement his status that I have to give him first look.

Bean puts time in his diary for him to walk the windows. It's taken us six months to get these windows right. In the ten minutes it'll take us to walk around the shop façade, I'll know if it was worth it. Curiously, I don't feel particularly nervous. I think it's because, while he holds the purse strings and so has the power, I can already tell that he has little understanding when faced with anything resembling contemporary installations. Antonia once raved about a Jackson Pollock exhibition at the Royal Academy, and he simply shook his head and muttered, 'Give me a Rembrandt any day.' Business growth and a well-tailored ZEGNA suit Ken might get, but anything abstract or conceptual leaves him confused. Not that I intend to let him know that's what I think.

'Dressed for a funeral, Mary?' Ken greets me brusquely. Perhaps I shouldn't have worn my Comme des Garçons coat.

Disciples of the Japanese designer Rei Kawakubo are called Little Crows, such is the amount of black she puts into her collections. Many critics don't get it, cruelly calling Comme des Garçons the 'Hiroshima bag lady look'. But I love the way she's made something so subversive still feel sexy. This sweeping floor-length coat, with its billowing sleeves and huge turn-up cuffs, makes me feel powerful. There's nothing cooler than that.

'I'd love to know your favourite window?' I say deferentially, trying to move Ken along. I have to dig deep into the skills that won me a place at RADA to act with the kind of respect he wants.

'The cherubs are a cute touch,' Ken replies somewhat predictably.

'Yes! Nothing says Christmas like a cherub, eh? As I learnt at my convent school,' I shoot back. Positioning myself as a good Catholic girl should surely help. I get the impression Ken grew up with that Middle American buttoned-upness, where Sunday school was de rigueur – even if it was more about scoring a future wife than points with God.

The next day Des calls in sick. 'I can't see a fucking thing,' he moans. All that glitter has given him conjunctivis.

Who needs laxatives?

IT'S THE TUESDAY BEFORE CHRISTMAS, which means we're expected in Ken's office at 3 p.m. for the monthly results. These meetings are never easy, a strange mixture of posturing and defensiveness. The team is jittery too because the fashion director of *The Times* has just written an article declaring 'The Department Store Is Dead'. Her argument is that, now designers like Dolce and Versace are opening their own Bond Street boutiques, the power of places like Harvey Nichols is waning. It's got everyone in a tizz. And I'm feeling it worse than most because this is also the meeting where we'll find out whether my Christmas windows did their job. 'Who needs laxatives when you've got this meeting to go to?' I grimace to Bean on my way out the door.

Antonia's jacket has shoulders sharper than my Stanley knife. She's trying to out-suit the men in the room and it works. Callum is putty in her hands, choosing to talk about Christmas plans rather than grill her on what she's bought for next season from the designers' annual Cruise shows – collections geared around wealthy women who seek out winter sun.

'We're heading to our place in Provence,' she says. 'It's a wreck. But the view? C'est magnifique.'

Antonia's been house-hunting in the South of France for years. She wouldn't admit it, but I suspect it's her way of building a home with Simon, her partner who's locked in an acrimonious divorce that's dragging on. Getting out of the first marriage has been so complicated, it's not looking likely he'll consider a second.

'It's a little tense at home,' Antonia admits, fiddling with her huge crucifix. I know enough about Antonia by now to know that's a sign she's nervous. But whether about the home front or the weekly numbers I'm not sure.

Ken doesn't hang about. He's flying back to Ohio tonight. 'Page three of your pack,' he instructs. 'We're up 4% against budget. Starting the festive shop earlier clearly worked. Menswear, down 3%. We took a hit on coats, with all the unseasonable weather. Shoes, down 4%, which needs looking at. Luckily, beauty's on fire. Up a whopping 15%. And womenswear – up 11% and 10% year on year. Eveningwear has been especially strong. Well done, Antonia. Those Frank Usher exclusives have delivered.'

'It helped they were in prime position in the windows, eh, Antonia?' Callum ventures. His jostling is as much because he doesn't want to be left out of the picture as it is a chance to give me some acknowledgement. But, still, I appreciate the gesture. 'Mary made them look the part.'

'I don't know about that,' Ken shoots back, speaking to Callum but looking directly at me. 'The Harrods windows looked much the same as ours. Only more Christmasy. Richer. Real class. I don't like following where others lead.'

There's a silence. I can feel myself burning up.

Driving home for Christmas

I'M PACKING UP FOR THE Christmas break when Callum peers around the door.

'Got something for you, Mary,' he grins, thudding a huge hamper onto my desk. 'Now don't you go beating yourself up about Ken. It's like pissing into the wind. We all know how much Harrods spend on their windows. If Ken wants ours to look richer, he'd better get his chequebook out.' He pats the hamper. 'You've made your mark this year,' he adds. 'Enjoy the break.'

I don't need to open it to know what it is. The black serif F&M painted on the top tells me this is from Fortnum & Mason. Legend has it that these hampers started in the eighteenth century, when wealthy customers stopped by Fortnum's to stock up for the long, horse-drawn carriage journey to their country estates. The Scotch eggs, boiled ham and fruit cake would see them through some questionable meals at the roadside inns along the way. I think there's another reason these are the Christmas gifts of choice from men like Callum, though. They remind them of the tuck boxes their mum would send them off to boarding school with. Still, I'm not complaining. Food is always a comfort to me. Christmas food even more so.

I should be pleased. But driving home for Christmas I feel empty.

It happens every year at this time of year. The excitement, the grief, the nostalgia and then the way my siblings and I pull together to celebrate Christmas. All our partners know the unspoken rule: Christmas will always be the Newtons, all together. We don't do in-laws because two of my brothers are single, so where would they go? And anyway we all take comfort in being together. It's our way of coping still. When Mum died, it felt like this was our shared nightmare – how could anyone else understand that? And so this band of five siblings has come together in oneness every year since.

Christmas was a time my mother made so wonderful. She wove all her love into making it special, and when we gather each year, we know it's because we want to hold on to that love and as much of her as we can.

Tish and I keep some of Mum's rituals alive. The Christmas cake has to be made in November, even though none of us actually enjoy eating it. We'll get together for Stir Up Sunday, pulling out Mum's now cocoa-stained recipe and her little plastic decorations – two reindeers and Santa in his sleigh. I keep them wrapped in her faded tissue paper, one little reindeer with the thick, snowy icing Mum had last made still attached to its hooves. Each year, the white fondant has hardened and crumbled, but the sentimental value only grows stronger. I can't throw it away.

I also have my Christmas cupboard of goodies like Mum used to do. Around November she would set aside a small portion of her grocery budget each week to start stockpiling, a little at a time. Our pantry slowly filled with non-perishables like dried fruits, mincemeat and sugar for Christmas baking, along with jars of jam, bottles of ginger wine, pickles, Twiglets, cheese straws and other festive treats. By spacing out these purchases over several months, she eased the financial strain of Christmas that came with having five kids.

I didn't need to, but I did the same. Graham would humour me by adding to my little stockpile, knowing how much this meant to me. This year, however, my cupboard has been elevated. Callum's Fortnum & Mason hamper is full of exoticism – candied chocolate-covered ginger, sugared chestnuts – and a grateful supplier has sent me some pretty impressive bottles of wine, with tips on how to store them horizontally in 60 to 70% humidity.

We're having Christmas at ours, but everyone in the family is responsible for bringing a dish. Graham and I do the turkey and all the trimmings. My sister Tish, the Brussels sprouts and Delia Smith's parsnips in parmesan. Joe's in charge of the red cabbage. Michael, the smoked salmon blinis. Lawrence, the cheese platter. Forever the baby, he's got the one thing that's less cooking, more assembly.

I see Joe pulling up in his little red MG midget as I'm putting the finishing touches to the dining table. The perks of the job are self-evident at this time of the year. I've been able to get the best of all the festive stock with my staff discount.

This year, I'm going natural. The centrepiece is a lush garland of fresh pine, eucalyptus and holly, which I've intertwined with strings of warm, glowing fairy lights and tapered candles from the Mulberry Home shop on the fourth floor. I love Mulberry Home and Roger Saul who designs it and remember Princess Anne coming to cut the ribbon when we launched. I thought it was funny she had worn her driving shoes, the right heel all scuffed up from some over-enthusiastic clutch action from bombing around Balmoral.

By the time we crack open Callum's bottle of vintage port, I'm tipsy enough to admit that things at work aren't as cheery as the tablescape. 'I'm exhausted,' I admit. 'I feel like I'm constantly putting on a front.' It's only now I'm here, back with my family, that it hits me quite how alone I feel. Senior enough to be excluded from the all-night rave Cass had organised for the display team as an alternative Christmas party, but not senior enough to be taken seriously by Antonia. Even the succession of work experience kids seemed to belong better than me. 'My mother's been friends with Antonella since they met at school in Switzerland,' I'd hear them say, interchanging the name of the Harvey Nichols staffer for whoever had leant into the nepotism hardest that month. The Baroque windows had been beautiful, but I knew they weren't drawing crowds, pushing boundaries. Too worried about the heritage of Harvey Nichols, too intimidated by the luxury elite, I was struggling to find my voice.

Start looking. Really looking

NEW YEAR, WORKING LATE AGAIN. The store is silent. The yellow light from my Nina Campbell lamp, warm. I'm taking a break from dictating memos for Bean to type up tomorrow, reading one of the books my predecessor had left on the shelves. It's about the history of window dressing and has a chapter on the artist Salvador Dalí, who caused a stir with his surrealist take for the windows of New York's department store Bonwit Teller in 1939. Apparently, the Upper West Siders hadn't been best pleased by his 'Narcissus Complex' display. In one, he'd had three wax hands holding mirrors reaching out of a lambskin-covered bathtub filled with water. In another, he'd replaced the feet of a four-poster bed with buffalo legs and plonked a head eating a pigeon on the canopy. Dalí was charged with disorderly conduct and the windows were tweaked, but that hadn't put off Andy Warhol, whose windows for Bonwit Teller in the 60s were considered his big break. I loved that these men had made windows a piece of art. I also loved how they'd made headlines — and history.

I've been so head down, I've stopped looking. I've been treating Harvey Nichols like it's a race, even though I've got no idea what the finish line looks like. But while activity comes from putting the hours in, progress — real progress — is about achieving something that goes deeper and touches people. And for that I needed some headspace. Time to be moved myself, by the creativity I saw in London's galleries, theatres, shops and clubs. Even the streets.

I ring Mandy, my old Topshop mucker. I want her opinion, her help reviewing the department store competition.

Once a month me and my old team at Topshop used to go on a window safari to see what the competition was doing. We didn't take much notice of the department stores. The fashion chains were who we focused in on. No one my age shopped in department stores, and I couldn't help but feel this may be part of the problem.

Mandy and I meet at Marble Arch, the scrubby end of Oxford Street, where street vendors hawk 'My mate came to London and all I got was this' T-shirts to tourists on their way to Buckingham Palace. Mandy's wearing a tartan skirt, with black leggings and a denim bomber jacket. Orange leg warmers are pulled up to her knees, a pair of Air Jordans just visible below them. She's puffing on a Silk Cut.

'I thought you'd stopped the fags, Mand,' I say.

'I basically have. I only do five a day now,' she grins, stubbing it out and giving me a hug.

I remember how we used to jump into the grimy, yellow-fogged smoking carriage on the train back home from Euston after work,

69

both lighting up before launching into our gossip from the day. I quit recently and have started running – a way to keep in check some of the jumpiness I've felt since starting at Harvey Nichols. But, seeing Mandy, I'm tempted to have 'just one'. I loved the days at Topshop that started with a Diet Coke, a fag and some peanut butter toast from the caff round the corner, the grease seeping through the paper bag. We came up with some of our best ideas then. And all before 9 a.m.

Mandy and I start at Selfridges. The building is magnificent: colonnades stretching up to a yellow flag that catches the sun just so. The windows are slick but samey. The mannequins are professionally styled – no stray thread distracting from the black dresses – but they hardly have the wow factor. Inside, though, it's heaving. 'Looks like they're mainly day trippers,' suggests Mandy as we wander the ground floor with its perfume halls, hosiery and hats. Fighting our way through the crowds on our Oxford Street crusade, we see it's a similar story at all the department stores. John Lewis . . . House of Fraser . . . Debenhams . . . D.H. Evans . . . Even Fenwick . . . All mammoth buildings, whose arching windows feel professional and classic, with mere, slight variations on theme. With competition like this, perhaps it won't actually take much to shake the market up? Or is this what the department store shopper feels comfortable with? It was easy for me and Mandy to create crazy Topshop windows because we were our target customer. We instinctively understood what girls wanted. This is so much harder.

It's shops like HMV that have people pouring out of them. The doors are open onto the street, music pumping out. I peer in and see people flicking through CD cases and putting head-phones on to stand, absorbed, in the albums they're sampling that day. 'Try before you buy . . .' I say to Mandy.

GAP has the same energy. The store is buzzing, with jazz playing. The cool young sales team wear crisp white T-shirts, denim jackets and khakis – a vibe that blends joy, style and a touch of effortless American confidence.

I need more inspiration. I might still not know the department store clientele, but I do know what makes shops or markets the places people want to hang in. The most successful make customers feel something – something more than what they sell. They make them want to be part of the place, to soak up the atmosphere.

Never turn down good advice. Or a good lunch

WHEN YOU'RE ATTUNED TO IT, inspiration comes from every-where – and everyone.

I'm at lunch with British *Vogue*'s Fashion Director Anna Harvey. We're at Launceston Place, the only restaurant amongst a row of Regency-style houses on a leafy Kensington Street. Despite its domestic location, or perhaps because of it, since Princess Diana started coming here it's impossible to get a table. The fact that we've managed it today has nothing to do with me. That's all Anna, who as well as styling the most richly evocative shoots at *Vogue* is Diana's personal stylist. She's taken her from a few fusty Laura Ashley blouses to the most recognised woman in the world – and British fashion's most powerful force. What Diana is seen wearing on the cover of *Hello!* magazine, women want to buy.

Anna would pooh-pooh such accolades. 'I just trundle over to KP with a few rails,' is how she puts it. But that's part of her charm.

It's not hard to see why Diana relies on her. She's got impec-cable style, of course – all minimalist tailoring and statement jewellery. And a curious mix of old-school formality and maternalism that sees me opening up to her.

She tells me fashion can be cruel. And to be taken seriously, I need to take myself seriously. 'As you should, dear girl. You have talent,' she tells me, folding her starched napkin neatly.

That means I need to address my wardrobe. Three things should be on my shopping list, she says: a white shirt − 100% cotton, stiff collar − any Yohji Yamamoto simple dress and Yves Saint Laurent's Le Smoking. The classic YSL suit will cost me a month's salary, she says, but it will pay off.

A junkyard in the window

I'T'S ON A TRIP TO the Whitechapel Gallery that I discover Carhenge. A series of photographs documents the installation in 1987 of a circle of vintage cars in the Nebraska desert. It's the work of Jim Reinders, an artist who wanted to build a memorial to his late father on the site of his farm. He spray-painted thirty-nine cars matte grey and organised them in a circle to look like Stonehenge, the prehistoric stones on Salisbury Plain. Some cars are sunk vertically into huge holes in the sand, some welded in place horizontally across two to make an archway. When Reinders was asked why he'd created Carhenge, his answer was simply, 'Why not?' It's eerie, odd . . . and beautiful. I can't stop looking at the images. Could this work as a window? It's mad. But it could be brilliant.

Getting the idea signed off by Callum and then Ken isn't as easy as the Baroque tableau had been. It's coming up to bonus season and Callum is twitchy. He's already put a hole in the roof of his huge pile nestled in the Chiltern hills, ready for work on the extension to begin when the cash hits in April. 'Susan's already measuring up the curtains,' he eye-rolls. But he agrees that I can take it to Ken. 'Be my guest,' he says. 'And then, if Ken goes for it, you can take it to Antonia. But I want to be there when she hears about the dust clouds that'll obscure her Cruise collections.'

I knew Ken would be difficult to swing. He boasted endlessly about American retail and New York's big department stores' successful windows. The British sense of humour and rebellion in my ideas often bypassed him, so I wasn't feeling confident about selling in windows that rivalled a junkyard. What I didn't yet know was that Ken was a car freak. 'Nebraska's answer to Stonehenge,' he says, as I turn around my mood board. 'It's unhenged.' He chuckles at his own joke. Turns out Ken has always wanted a vintage Cadillac. 'Well, you can take the one from window 12 when we dismantle the display,' I joke. 'Then it's a done deal,' he shoots back, in all seriousness.

Constructing the windows isn't quite as simple. Jesus is quick to warn that we can't use real cars as they'll be too heavy to stand up. And if they crash down and out the front windows, we would all be out of a job. Also, we might kill someone. We find a factory so full of grit it makes your eyes sting, but they're able to create fibreglass models of car bodies; we'll top and tail these models with the real thing. I send Cass to every scrap-metal place inside the M25. I hazard she'll be best placed to sweet-talk the owners into giving us some bits for free. I'm right. Doors, fenders and bonnets start piling up in the loading bay, ready to be painted. There's no way we can hide this from Antonia. 'Mais non! You can't be serious, Mary. This is ghastly.' She confronts me in the corridor, twisting her crucifix as if she hopes it'll miraculously open into a bottle of vodka. 'Chanel has just shown their Cruise collection in the Grand Palais and you're hoping to put the pieces I've bought from that amongst a Steptoe and Son-style rag-and-bone junkyard.'

I need to have Antonia on board, to make her feel part of the process. 'It's very of the moment, Antonia. I love the juxtaposition of industrial meeting your streamlined collection,' I try, taking her through the visuals, asking her advice on the clothes she thinks could work within it, the colour schemes. 'I think that grey should be more of a lilac,' she ventures. 'You're right. That's a great idea, thank you,' I shoot back, keen to appease.

Des and Donald need managing with almost as much care. They've turned up in my office unannounced, on their usual mission: they want new mannequins.

At Topshop, we had cheap mannequins. You had to cut a hole in the sole of the shoe you were using — usually an ugly, cheap court shoe or a job lot of jelly flats and Converse — to wrestle it onto the mannequin. You couldn't do that at Harvey Nichols, ruining a perfectly sellable £200 pair of Emma Hope kitten heels in the process. Which is why we turned to Rootstein, the queen of mannequin makers.

Born to Russian parents, Adel Rootstein had started out as a window dresser for Aquascutum on Oxford Street. Anticipating the demand for fashionable display props, she'd set up Rootstein in the 50s, working with sculptor John Taylor on creating forms that told a story about what was going on in fashion. The day's top models, from Twiggy in the 60s to Yasmin Le Bon in the 80s, would come into her West Kensington studio to be sculpted into mannequins that so beautifully captured their movement, their poise, their stance.

So many tried to copy Adel Rootstein, so many undercut. But nobody was as good. My favourite was her Lazy Lizzie collection, nonchalant, slouched and super cool. You knew the premium price was worth it. On a Rootstein, you could just drop a dress over and it would look exquisite.

'The problem is,' says Donald calmly, 'we just can't find the right poses amongst the mannequins we've got in the stockroom. We could really do with the X10. You know, hands straight down. They're stark, simple and just so right for the scheme, don't you think?' As the longest-serving, most rational member of the display team, he's clearly been volunteered to present the case to me.

'OK,' I agree. 'It's Q1. Let's blow the budget.'

Even the Rootstein showroom is chic. Adel is known for her elaborate set-ups, designed to best show off her new mannequins. Today, her brilliant creative director Kevin Arpino has arranged them around a life-size swimming pool, the alabaster skin reflecting brightly off the water. As we walk around, we discuss what skin tone we want the mannequins sprayed with (a peach melba, that'll stand out against the grey), what make-up would work best (smoky and unsubtle) and hair (a blunt bob).

We're not insured to dress the windows out of hours, so construction starts early one Wednesday morning. The ladies-who-lunch brigade can't work out what's going on as my team haul the car parts they've sanded and painted through the shop floor, ready to be nailed into place. When a stray wing mirror sends a pile of Chanel alligator bags clattering to the floor, they flee.

Des and Donald are oblivious to the carnage as they hammer the car pieces in place. Donald's been off sick for a few days: one of his migraines, which seem to regularly floor him. It's hard to know how to tackle it with him. Donald's always been so private. He gives little away.

'How you been, mate?' I hear Des asking him as I come down from my office to check up on progress. 'You know, you can talk to her if you need to,' he adds softly.

Donald nods but stays silent. The pair rake sand across the floor covering their footprints as they back out to exit the display. I pretend I've just arrived, and together we walk onto the street to survey the scene. The lights have been rigged to make it look like sunset at Carhenge: the deep oranges giving the grey cars a ghoulish feel. Against the feeling of emptiness, the monochrome mannequins peeping out from behind the cars are glowing. Surely even Antonia is going to have to agree the mix of power suits and swimsuits looks sharp.

Shame

'WHAT THE FUCK IS THIS, Mary?' Ken says, backing off the pavement and into the road to look up at the grey Chevrolets that fill the front windows. He's furious and instantly makes me feel small.

'It was an exhibition at the Whitechapel Gallery that inspired me. I thought it would make an interesting and unusual combination,' I start uncertainly.

'I wasn't asking for a blow by fucking blow account,' Ken interrupts. 'I was asking why you've built a Detroit ghost town in the front of our store. What about this says luxury? We're supposed to be selling four-figure-sum suits, not turning Knightsbridge into some kind of a junkyard. Does Antonia know about this?'

'Erm, she saw me working on it, but I don't think she's seen the final installation. I'm so sorry, Ken,' I stumble. 'I thought I made it clear it was a riff on Carhenge when we talked about the plans.'

'You showed me cars,' he replies testily. 'Automobiles. The promise of freedom, of open roads, of the American dream. Not this. How long are these meant to be in place? This is not what this business needs. It's a fucking insult to the store.'

I get off the bus a stop earlier for the next six weeks so I can walk through Lowndes Square and avoid the windows. Looking at them makes me feel nauseous. I feel an overwhelming weight pressing down on my heart, an uncomfortable mix of embarrassment and inadequacy.

I know that the rumours have gone round the store – Portas has fucked up royally. I start to imagine the talk. 'How can some upstart from Watford understand luxury?' they'll whisper.

As a Catholic kid, I'm well aware of the power of shame. However, this feels different. This time I feel fear, especially at night. The endless loop in my head that tells me I'm an outsider and that Ken not only doesn't like me but doesn't even rate me. I knew Ken couldn't stand the fact that Sir Peter had put me here. I wasn't his choice. I certainly wasn't his type of person. It made me feel uncomfortable just being in his presence. He knew that. And now my worry was he would sack me.

'It's *Vogue* calling . . .'

'WELL, WELL, WELL,' SAYS CALLUM, rapping on my office door and throwing a copy of *Retail Week* on my desk. The lead story on page three is about Carhenge. I hesitate, searching Callum's face for clues, before I take it in. 'Innovative Windows Rev Up Harvey Nichols' is the headline. The story reports that cars have been stopping in the middle of Sloane Street so drivers can peer through the windows of their Audis and BMWs at our rusty Carhenge. 'Who said department stores are dead, eh?' laughs Callum. 'Good job, Mary. I'm looking forward to hearing what other crazy ideas you're cooking up next.'

Ken says nothing to me about the fact that the windows are getting rave reviews. Even when Antonia lets slip in a board meeting that the charismatic new boss at Selfridges had approached the pair of them at a recent dinner to congratulate them on the Carhenge coup, Ken is steely. 'Well, he came from Habitat, so nuts and bolts might make sense to him. But they don't work for me,' he sneers.

I wish it didn't, but his scorn spurs me on. I so want to prove him wrong. So often in business, validation comes not from your bosses but from peers – people you respect and vie with. Those are the people I want to impress.

Weekly brainstorms take on a new energy as our window schemes become more talked about. Callum has taken it upon himself to deal with Ken – and, I realise, cheerlead on my behalf. It's easier to back up my work when the likes of *Vogue* and *ELLE Decoration* are turning up to a host of events each time we unveil a window.

For the opening of London Fashion Week, my carpentry team create to-scale models of the capital's most iconic landmarks, which we subvert and spray-paint in fluorescent colours, getting giddy off the smell. Hot pink pigeons. Nelson, wearing a Westwood frock, astride a bent-out-of-shape replica of his column.

Some windows caused a kerfuffle. For a scheme dedicated to British icons, we raided charity stores and bought second-hand fridges, sofas, dining tables, ironing boards, tea sets, rugs, anything that created a room set. We then sprayed every item in one colour – a baby pink. Then, when the installation looked one-dimensional and weirdly surreal, we painted the faces of famous Brits onto them. David Bowie's face on a sofa, Michael Caine on a wardrobe. One famous model has complained we've put her on an ironing board. 'I don't want girls to get the wrong impression that I'm really thin. Flat as an ironing board. It's not a good message,' she'd telephoned Antonia to protest. 'Tell her I can get Ruth to paint her on a double-doored wardrobe instead,' Des eye-rolls when I report back. 'That'll shut her up.'

Some windows were just beautiful. Inspired by a Picasso exhibition I'd fallen in love with, I decided to cover his blue period and style the mannequins only in navy blue. We painted every square foot of the windows a rich Yves Klein blue. We had to remix the paint five times to get the perfect colour: it exuded a powerful, almost meditative beauty as the navy mannequins appeared as subtle silhouettes, both mesmerising and monochromatic.

Soon, all of the windows get us talked about. The trade magazine *Drapers* spends six weeks covering the installation of our latest shoe windows for a cover story. And then I get a call from *Vogue*. 'They want to shoot you for a double-page spread,' Bean squeals into my office before transferring the call, somewhat ruining the surprise. 'And it's for the September issue.' The biggest pagination of the year, the September issue previews the autumn/winter collections. These are the clothes luxury bosses need to sell across the peak shopping season, which is why they invest in magazine advertising to secure premium slots in the glossiest of *Vogue's* fashion shoots. Bean is practically hopping with excitement. 'Can I come on set? I think you might need me.'

I know Anna Harvey is behind my *Vogue* moment, and so, that morning, I choose an outfit I think she'll approve of: a simple baby-pink Claude Montana waistcoat and cigarette pant, paired with a thick black roll neck to make it look sharp, not saccharine. Her guidance has seeped into so much of my wardrobe, anyway. I've stripped back the crazy colours and shoulder pads in favour of a sleeker look. I've realised my height isn't something to hide. I've cropped my hair short. It feels less fussy.

And – bonus – means I don't have to spend precious time each morning styling it.

The *Vogue* team arrives en masse at Harvey Nichols. I'm always surprised by how many people there are on set: from the scowling photographer who's all about 'the art' to the poor girl who's currently unpacking and steaming the creases out of clothes to fill a rail that will barely be touched. 'Darling, that's fabulous! You persuaded Galliano to send the samples in the end then,' coos stylist Isabella Blow as she moves hangers around to create outfits she'll try to convince me to change into. It's all asymmetric shapes and flamboyant prints – outrageous looks. But what else would you expect from Issy? She's gone from Anna Wintour's assistant to the barometer for who and what's hot in fashion now. Legend has it Andy Warhol became obsessed with Issy when he noticed her odd Manolo Blahnik shoes – one pink, one purple. And today she's still dressing like an eccentric aristo who's been disinherited. In other words, exactly who she is.

After *Vogue* hits the newsstands, Brian Sewell, the *Evening Standard*'s art critic, starts reviewing the opening of our windows. 'There is more art in Harvey Nichols than the Whitechapel Gallery,' he writes. I suspect it's as much a dig at the Whitechapel's curator as an endorsement of us, but no matter – I'll take it.

But it's when Antonia makes an appointment to talk to me about Callum that I know the windows are really landing. It's the first time she's sought out my opinion, wanted me as an ally.

Callum has made the concession business his top priority:

seeking out labels he can charge big money for the privilege of being on the shop floor. And he's good at it: the deals are rolling in, brand installations popping up in every department. They get the credibility of being in Harvey Nichols; we get revenue per square foot of their installation as well as a cut of their sales. It's a no-brainer, as Callum is fond of saying.

As a business strategy, I understand it: the up-front, financial security of concessions helps mitigate the risk that comes from Antonia and her team of buyers. Their job is to attend designer catwalk shows, then go to examine the collections up close in the studios, scrutinise line-sheets and buy what they think the Harvey Nichols woman will want to shop in six months' time. Our 'own buy' from designers was down to Antonia and her team's eye, instinct and relationships. But it was also a gamble. If the stock didn't sell, there was no return on investment, and the entire business suffered. I often wondered how Antonia coped with the pressure and the peril.

But if Callum's concessions were the cash cows that kept the lights on, the overheads paid, they were – more often than not – the B team brands. Labels that the designers Antonia wooed wouldn't want to be associated with.

Antonia had caught wind of a new wave coming in and was livid. I understood why. Her argument was that the power of Harvey Nichols came from a clever, eclectic edit. Creating a place where people would come for a bit of a wander and discover new names, new ideas. And a place where, in turn, concessions would pay to be cool by association. If Callum messed with that cycle too much, Antonia feared, it would all come crumbling down.

'Callum, c'est horrible.' Antonia dives into his proposals in our weekly catch-up. 'You must see what this will look like to the industry. I've worked too hard to build up our reputation to let this happen.' She looks at me purposefully, raising her eyebrows as my cue to back her up.

'I think what Antonia's trying to say is that while we totally understand the necessity of concessions, they need to be ring-fenced,' I try diplomatically. Callum's still my boss.

'Girls, this is a numbers game. And we need to hit them,' Callum says, shutting us down. 'Besides, when did you two start playing for the same team?'

Antonia was smart enough to see that my changes were working. She wanted to be part of that success. I hoped she was also beginning to understand that I loved so much of what she fiercely stood for. Was appreciative that, for the first time, there was finally someone in the sales department who wasn't merely about shifting the product she'd carefully curated for the shop floor, but actually giving it a platform with creativity, care and flair.

But I was also learning that, behind Antonia's posturing, there was a woman, like me, trying to find her space in an alpha-dominated world. Her approach was to quote operas or ballets she'd popped into the night before. Mine was to create a world they couldn't understand. To move the creativity into a space that was so far removed from their confined structures and strategy that they almost had no choice but to just let me be. 'I don't get it,' Callum would often say. 'But go for it.' His trust gave me the space I needed.

Mean girls (and men)

A BUSINESS BUILT ON HIERARCHY finds various ways to put you in your place, the subtler, the better.

Walk the shop floor and you can tell there's a new buzz around Harvey Nichols. But up on our floor, it's hard to feel any excitement. Management is preoccupied by news that the store is being sold: our new owner is a Hong Kong billionaire we are to call Chairman.

He's flying into London for the weekend to inspect his new asset. We're expected to make it look worth the £53.6 million he paid for it. And make sure we hold on to our jobs.

It's Sunday, and we've been summoned to the office. No mention of the fact that it's a weekend. Or of getting any extra pay. The Chairman wants 'the big picture', so Ken's asked for directors to present on everything from the store merchandising to sales budgets and the buying breakdown. As Head of Display, I'm a mere head of department, but Callum has dragged me away from a weekend of DIY with Graham as he wants me to sit in on the sales segment at the board meeting and explain the upcoming windows and store designs. 'I'll take the Chairman through the numbers, the strategy, the big picture,' he instructs. 'Then you can do the specifics on the windows.' I'd like to think it's because Callum knows he'd do a crap job at selling in some of the madcap schemes I've got planned. But it also crosses my mind that he might want a fall guy if it all starts going Pete Tong.

The office is freezing. Without the bustle and gossip of everyone else, it feels empty and echoing. I've been at my desk for hours, waiting for the call to head to the boardroom. We weren't told what time we'd be on stage, but I have no doubt we'll be kept waiting. There's no way Ken will wrap up a meeting that's over-running in front of the Chairman. He'll be too busy crapping it.

I leaf through my board papers again, highlighting the facts I want to get across. It's lunchtime. I'm restless, stressed . . . and starving.

'I'm just popping to the vending machine,' I say to Bean, who's so bored she's brought out her knitting. Her grandpa lives in what *Tatler's* described as 'the coldest house in England', so Bean's taken it upon herself to make indoor scarves for her poor old ma and pa who've been roped into monetising the place. 'I won't be long. But come and find me if you get the call.'

The vending machine's on the floor above, at the end of a long corridor. I pass Antonia's office, peering in to see if she wants anything. It's empty. Callum's too. Where are they all?

By the time I reach Ken's office upstairs, it's clear something's going on. His PA, Sylvia, sits outside, standing guard. 'Where is everyone?' I ask. Sylvia blushes, fumbling as she says they've gone out for lunch. 'Oh, why didn't you call for me?' I ask before my brain kicks in. Because I already know the answer. She had a list of names to summon. Mine wasn't on it.

I know I'm not a director but this feels so painful. Alienation. Abandonment. A visceral reminder that I'm not one of them.

I hit the vending machine and keep walking, down the stairs and out onto Sloane Street. It's baltic and I haven't got my coat. But I keep walking, through the pristine streets of Knightsbridge. Without really knowing where I'm going, I find myself at the *Dancers* sculpture in Cadogan Square. It's a place I sometimes come to eat lunch when I need some peace. I love the energy of the two naked dancers, their bodies intertwined. The bronze is slowly turning that oxidised green.

I spot Elspeth, sitting cross-legged on the grass by the statue. One of the area's few homeless, we'd first met months before when I'd disturbed her rifling around the skip in the loading bay on my way home after working late one night. She was looking for anything that'd been discarded from the window display that she could use for bedding. She'd told me her name was Elspeth. Scottish for Elizabeth, she'd added, meaning 'chosen by God'. 'I've never worked out what he's chosen me for,' she'd laughed. 'Maybe to show the rich folk around here how they've landed on their friggin' feet.' I told her I had an English teacher called Elspeth who had a lisp. 'Elthpeth,' she cackled as she pulled out cracked silver PVC stars we'd chucked away. 'These'll cheer up my wee spot,' she said as she wandered off, stars tucked under her arms.

I'm not sure why but I end up telling Elspeth about my shitty day. She listens. And then scrambles around in a Sainsbury's bag and hands me a sprig of heather. 'It's hardy. Just like yous.'

Weeks later, the morning before my window walk with Ken, I'm scrambling around at the bottom of my bag for some lipstick. There's nothing like a slick of red to fake confidence. Instead of an Estée Lauder bullet though, I find a twiggy bit of Elspeth's heather. Most of the sprig has crumbled into the lining. Even with a good shake, it'll never quite come out. But as I rub the nub between my thumb and fingers, I feel resolve. Fuck you lot, I think. Keep your pasta carbonara. It'll take more than being left out of lunch to put me down.

Hope is powerful. So is a Rifat Ozbek jacket

I T'S MY FIRST TIME IN Germany since the fall of the Berlin Wall. I'm in Düsseldorf for the annual display and visual merchandising trade fair. It's a chance to see innovations in props, interior display units and new style mannequins. Plus to party.

I'm wearing my Rifat Ozbek jacket. My wardrobe's sizeable these days, but this is — hands down — the best thing in it right now. Turkish-born and London-based Ozbek knows how to cut a jacket so it fits to perfection. What I love about it is that the masculine, military style is offset by the soft velvet and the rich colour: a beautifully vibrant Yves Klein bluey purple, with navy cuffs separated by a gold trim. The bodice is laced with ceramic made to look like bones. It's impossible to ignore, often sparking unexpected conversations with the most interesting of strangers. It makes me feel like Boudica.

This year there's a different energy to the event, and I don't think it's just because of my jacket. It's the sense of hope that is in the air. It feels like the place is flooded with it.

Hope is so vital in society. The brilliant American theologian and journalist Krista Tippett, who spent many years living in West Berlin, describes hope as a muscle. You need to keep using it. Her theory goes that hope is generative; it propels us forward. I love that theory. We're energised not by what we do day in and day out, but by the promise of what's to come. Hope is what's behind every big change in society. Without it we might survive, but we won't flourish.

Blonde ambition

WHENEVER I NEED AN ESCAPE, I head to the design studio on the roof. With panoramic views of London, you'd often find the team taking a break to smoke a spliff and sunbathe. Donald would tease me in a camp cockney Kenneth Williams voice whenever I tried to join them. I was their boss. But they were my people. I needed allies.

Today, music is blaring out and I walk in to see Cass teaching a poker-faced Donald the dance routine for Madonna's 'Vogue'. It's the summer of 1990, and Madonna is part-way through her Blonde Ambition tour. The conical bra has stolen the headlines, but for my team the question they're most interested in is: 'What red lipstick has that much staying power?'

The answer, they tell me, is Russian Red. It's made by MAC, a beauty line that's become cult amongst models, actors and now musicians for its staying power under studio lighting. One of the co-founders, Canadian Frank Toskan, was a make-up artist who found himself struggling to keep make-up looking punchy on film and in photography so decided to create his own. Together with marketing genius Frank Angelo, the pair have taken the business from their kitchen tables to one of the most buzzed-about brands. The New York store, with transvestites on the counter, regularly gets shut down so Michael and La Toya Jackson can shop there in peace.

'Jude's been trying to get Greta to launch MAC here, but she's not having it,' reports Cass. 'Stupid cow.' She tells me that Jude – a young assistant beauty buyer whose special skill is sniffing out newness – has been desperately trying to get a meeting in with the two Franks. 'It's audacious, sexy and exactly what we should be stocking,' Jude tells me.

The only problem? Her boss, Greta Barron, the Perfumery Buying Director, doesn't agree.

In charge of everything to do with the beauty hall, Greta's working day started with a fag, a coffee and an appointment at Hair by Harvey's on the fourth floor. There, amongst the peach dried floral arrangements, Vincenzo, in his sausage-casing black PVC trousers weaved his magic on teasing up her chignon and spraying industrial amounts of Elnett to deliver her signature hard-hat, helmet hairdo. Her next appointment would be lunch with one of the men who ran the fragrance houses – Estée Lauder, Guerlain, Dior – and then afternoon tea with another. Evening events required full-length mink with accompanying cigarette holder. In between, Greta would rest on a chaise longue in her office, barking commands at long-serving, longer-suffering Jude. I don't know how Jude puts up with Greta, but I'm glad she does.

Jude looks like she belongs in an episode of *The Clothes Show*, always in a bandana or a beret, but it's beauty that's her real passion. She's the one who's introduced me to Clinique's Black Honey; half lipstick, half lip gloss, I'm hooked on the brown shade that's selling point is that it suits everyone. And I'm not the only one. It's flying off the shelves.

Aside from the It cream that was Crème de la Mer — so cult I'd often detour via the beauty hall first thing in the morning to steal a £17-worth dollop from the sample on display and whack it on my face before doing my make-up at my desk — fragrance was where the money was at. Beauty houses seemed to launch a new 'prestige' bottle more often, it felt, than Cass washed her sheets. And, unlike fashion, there were big budgets involved. If only they'd come with imaginative ideas. Greta would often scuttle up to my office to report back from her latest lunch. 'Dior need a fresh push on Poison. It's wonderfully gothic, I'm not sure why it's been so divisive. Seduces you from the first whiff. Lots of plum, hints of coriander and anise. A touch of tuberose and those lingering base notes of musk, sandalwood and cedarwood. And, you'll know, of course, the Hypnotic bottle's a red apple. A play on Snow White, you see?' she'd rattle off. 'So we're thinking windows filled with plums and apples. Maybe one red one, half bitten, perched on top. Juicy but dangerous.' There wasn't much point in me trying to dissuade her. The beauty houses spent enough cash with us to afford them the final say. I hated the fact that just because some dry bloke at the top of Lauder had paid for the windows, he'd get to sign off on my ideas. Sponsorship felt wrong to me. But, for Greta, obsequiousness came naturally.

So entrenched in a world that had run much the same way for decades, Greta was fabulously disdainful of the new. She was having enough trouble understanding why her team were desperate to launch Aveda or Origins, brands mixing botanicals with beauty for the first time. 'A charcoal mask?' I heard Greta screeching to Jude when I ventured down to her office to discuss MAC. 'Charcoal's for the fireplace, not your face.'

Jude's asked me to help get Greta over the line. All we want, we argue, is a meeting with the Franks. 'Fine. Go, then. But if you think we're having transvestites in this beauty hall, you've got another . . .' she says, flouncing off in a trail of heady scent.

Next morning, we're on a flight to Canada determined to land the exclusive.

They don't wear slap like this in Harrods

I ARRIVE IN THE SNOW to MAC's offices on the outskirts of Toronto. I don't know what to expect but it's not a nose-ringed receptionist with bright pink hair, wearing a slip dress – all the better for showing off his sleeve of tattoos.

I soon come to realise that this is how Frank and Frank run the place: seeking out individuals, creatives with high energy and off-the-wall ideas, and then letting them run with them. Out the back, elderly women sit around a long table carefully slotting the lipstick bullets into the black cases. 'If our motto is "All ages, all races, all sexes", then our people need to be that too,' Angelo explains over coffee, stroking the Irish Setter that's drooling on his knee. Even the dogs around here are beautiful.

Together, they tell us the story of MAC, how Toskan had started developing make-up that reflects well on camera and works on all skin tones out of necessity. 'It was all just so wishy-washy and one note,' he recalls. 'So I started experimenting. And I'm a control freak so one thing led to another.' His first product was a non-reflective matte lipstick that didn't glare under a lens, but today it is products like the Spice lip liner that are hot. Rumour has it model Linda Evangelista loves the brown pencil so much she'll nip to the loo before a shoot starts so she can shove it on top of whatever the make-up artist has cooked up. Sales for Russian Red are also through the roof. 'We've got Debi to thank for that,' says Angelo, of Madonna's make-up artist. 'She knew Madge wouldn't be able to reapply mid-show with all that voguing going on, so Frank made her one that won't budge.'

It's anecdotes like this that Angelo, a businessman who's already created and sold multiple start-ups, has managed to capitalise on so brilliantly. He's grown MAC from Toskan's pet project into a million-dollar brand, but crucially without sacrificing its values. 'Everyone said launching a beauty store in SoHo was mad, but the New York gays love us,' he cackles.

Their energy is infectious. And validation of my belief that creativity will always win, that great business starts with ideas. So I start throwing ideas out to get them excited, and into Harvey Nichols. 'We'll have a launch party and invite all the dancers from The Edge,' I suggest. 'You can smear Russian Red all over the Hans Crescent windows.' We're still riffing at 2 a.m. over tequila in Toronto's only gay bar. They're game. God knows how we now get Ken over the line.

Money's the answer of course. MAC famously don't advertise anywhere, and they won't pay for windows. They believe their product is strong enough to make people come. And the numbers back them up. Frank and Frank have given us spreadsheets of the revenue they're taking in the New York store each quarter. It's staggering. 'We'll be the only retailer stocking MAC in the UK,' Jude makes the case to Ken and Greta. 'People will come from all over the country to get their hands on it. We'll see numbers like the New York ones.'

It's quite the promise, but she's not wrong.

A month later, we're down on the shop floor, waiting for the Franks and their team to arrive. Greta is reorganising the bottles of Loulou Cacharel on one of the counters; the hexagonal shape of the blue bottle means it's tricky to get them in a straight line. It offends her sense of order. I watch Jude scuttling towards us, flustered. She suddenly realises she's got no make-up on and stops to dip into the samples on display. The eyeshadow palettes are as dusty as the fake greenery trailing from the hanging baskets that are only allowed because they paid so much for their concession space. She knows the make-up will look terrible, but she also knows she can't turn up in front of Greta bare-faced.

The doors from Sloane Street swing open. Frank's in front, like the Pied Piper; behind him a cackling crew of drag queen make-up artists who've come from the US to staff the counter for the launch. Dressed in micro shorts and Vivienne Westwood-style SEX stilettos, their slicked skin gleams under the lights. They've added leather bondage-style aprons, paired with over-the-elbow gloves and baker boy hats. Their lipstick is purple, black or blood-red.

Within days, Miss Selfridge-clad kids are flocking to the beauty hall to spend £12 on an item they believe will transform them into a new persona. We're selling a Spice lip liner every eight minutes. No matter that for most of the people who buy it, the tawny colour is at least five shades darker than their lips. The key is to pair it with a lighter, milky lip gloss. Preferably, a MAC lustreglass. And be grateful disposable cameras make everything look a bit blurry.

Stefan, the front-loader thief

I'M TAKING A SHORTCUT THROUGH the scarf department on my way to see Ken, when Beatrice Dunhead, the shop-floor manager, stops me. Lanky, with sleek black hair pulled into a low tight bun, my team has nicknamed her Olive Oyl.

'Can I have a word, Mary?' she says, a sentence no one needs to hear when they're late for a meeting. She's just done her monthly stock take, and there's stuff missing. Specifically silk scarves signed out by my team supposedly for a window display.

'If they don't come back, I'm going to have to charge you the retail price,' she warns. 'And I hope when they do come back,' she adds, 'there's a reasonable explanation for their prolonged absence.'

Theft is commonplace in retail. At Topshop, no one really noticed a few cheap samples going astray. But at Harvey Nichols it's different. A girl in the shoe department has just been let go. She'd been pilfering new shoes, replacing them with her own scuffed pairs so that the boxes wouldn't feel suspiciously light. It caused quite a kerfuffle when a customer came in asking to try Rayne's latest collection. Peeling away layers of tissue paper embossed with the Royal Warrant, she expected to find black suede low-heeled court shoes, a dramatic chiffon and diamanté bow decorating the toe. Not a pair of worn burgundy creepers, rain-stained soles peeling away.

Four of the girls who work in PR have also been hauled in for questioning. The suspicion is they've been stealing samples. I can't help but feel a bit sorry for them as I watch security sweep their desks for evidence. Their jobs require them to be public facing: dinners, cocktails and coffees with members of the press who are being sent freebies from designers constantly. No doubt, the team also sees the bags arriving in the post room for Antonia as they're ferrying urgent samples back and forth to shoots, often on foot. The budget only stretches to one courier drop a day, and *Vogue*'s fashion editors don't like to be lumped in with everyone else. Can you blame them if they occasionally book out samples to wear for a work event? If, when that goes unnoticed, borrow one or two for a weekend too?

It's easy to tell the shop-floor manager you need to take something from the shop floor for a shoot. If they de-tag it great; but if not, there are ways. 'I'm from the press team. Just checking the windows quickly,' they'll tell the security guard, flashing their lanyard, to explain the bleeping as they leave the building and head to Heaven. Many nights the pieces will be missing less than twelve hours because they'll stumble back into work in the early hours to sleep off the booze in the fashion cupboard. It's warm there, and central. Saves them a night bus home or twenty quid on a black cab. They've learnt to slip the security guard a beauty bag for his missus every so often, so he turns a blind eye. They're regulars at the dry cleaner around the corner, who's a miracle worker at getting rid of a rogue sweat stain.

When a few people get away with it, others start. And while the behaviour might not be acceptable, it becomes endemic: a dissolution of moral boundaries. Only now Beatrice and her team are cracking down. It's being called theft, not just 'something that happens'.

Luckily the PR girls aren't my problem, but I do need to confront Des who heads up the windows where Beatrice's silk scarves were apparently headed. I've heard rumours that the display boys have been stuffing expensive socks and scarves down the front of their vintage Levi's. Effective technique. All the better if it makes them look well-endowed.

Ding-dong! The witch is dead

THERE ARE RUMBLINGS THAT THATCHER'S going to finally be toppled today. There have been rumours before, of course. Last time I was in New York, the buyer at Barneys – a department store going through a similar transformation to us – was asking me about her. 'I don't get it. She's amazing,' he drawled. 'Britain's finally booming. If she was American, we'd be carving her face into Mount Rushmore along with the greats.'

I understood his point of view. Thatcher had just been at the UN Global Summit, where world leaders (all men) gathered, as much to puff themselves up as talk politics. I'd watched her stride onto the stage and position herself right in the centre. Her punchy royal-blue suit making her as visible as the Queen in a sea of grey men. Part of me loved her for that. Power is sexy. No wonder most of the men at the top of retail were desperate to get an invite to her famous annual Downing Street drinks celebrating British business.

Perhaps it sounds strange, but I've never really felt like I had time for politics. I've been too busy surviving, building a life for myself. And, yes, I suppose I can now acknowledge, benefiting from much that Thatcher introduced. I grew up in a Labour household through and through; none of us would ever have even thought of voting Conservative. But I also grew up in a decade where you'd get used to the lights going out and not coming back on until morning. The miners' strike was in full swing, most around me were down to a three-day week, work – and life – restricted by power and energy.

So the 80s, with Reagan on one side of the pond and Thatcher on the other – all Wall Street, money, money, money – had felt like a gear shift. Like sitting in the front of a car and feeling that surge forwards when someone puts their foot down. London felt like it was booming: economically and culturally. And I was thriving, catapulted steeply into a very different lifestyle from the one I'd grown up in.

Many of my peers felt the foil of these boom times: a punkish anger, a determination to fight through the system. But that wasn't me. My theory, whether right or wrong, is that it's people who feel very safe, or people who feel very unsafe and have literally nothing to lose, who can risk protesting. I craved security, not anger. I was busy repairing the grief of my mother's death and father's abandonment by doing all I could to feel safe again – and filling my life with progression, hope and optimism. Finding a home, both literally and in Harvey Nichols. Perhaps it was naïve. But it was the only way I knew how to survive.

But increasingly – in this world where I see the differences between the people who have and the people who don't – I've begun to realise that politics isn't just this abstract thing. You've got Cass, who lives in a council flat six flights of stone steps up in Kenton. 'I've got mates in Trellick Tower. Love the view, but you can't get out in under fifteen minutes if it all kicks off,' she'd say, with a shrug. It's hardly a surprise that she's booking out the most expensive N.Peal cashmere socks to use in her display because she knows that after she's cut holes in them to get them over the spigot holding the mannequin in place she'll be able to keep them. 'Lush, these are,' she says, prancing around the studio.

Des hates Thatcher. He's watched her policies decimate the manufacturing industry in Huddersfield where he grew up. So many Northern towns have suffered, while here in our London bubble, we thrive. I can understand why my team are angry. 'You think fashion is drama? I can show you drama. Come home with me. Have a look at the dole queue, then have a look at the homophobia. I have to look at both every time I'm back there.'

I'm working through budgets in my office when I hear Bean fussing outside. 'She said she's not to be disturbed,' she hisses at Donald and Des. Bean's right: I really could do without the Double Ds trying to talk me into one of their schemes. I'd given them the opportunity to work up mood boards for next summer's display and they'd come back with seascapes – hardly an original idea. 'Well, it's always been popular before,' Donald had said grumpily, another little dig to remind the room he'd been around the block more times than me. But when I look up there's no strident Des, with curled lip. Instead, he holds out a bottle of vodka. 'Ding-dong! The witch is dead,' he sings triumphantly, waving the first edition of the *Evening Standard*. 'Thatcher Resigns' screams the front page. '"It's a funny old world," says tearful Premier,' the news report starts. Bean finds the delicate Spode china cups, borrowed from her auntie's flat in Kensington, and we drink shot after shot. Better times are coming.

Home is where the heart (and money) is

Between the successful Baroque Christmas windows and beginning to win over Antonia with my ideas, not just my adoption of Joseph jackets, I am finally feeling like I have found my place at this crazy store in the heart of posh Knightsbridge.

And the more I feel at home, the more I find myself wanting to create a home. Not a schmaltzy kind of home, but a wonderful feeling of aliveness in the store. Like a great market on a busy day where the air is filled with the hum of people, I feel there should be an energy pulsing through the floors.

So Callum, Antonia and I have come to New York to try and land some exclusives for a revamp of the fourth-floor homeware department. Americans do homeware so well, and the customer is spending big on the category. It makes sense: home ownership is baked into that stereotypical American sense of aspiration. We saw it in the 50s with the fetishisation of the housewife – pinny tied neatly in a bow, knocking up a gin cocktail for her husband coming home. The landscape's changed, but that idea of making a house a home is still prevalent today. The American dream that's being peddled invariably includes a house with colonnades, a white picket fence or a wraparound porch. And retailers have sprung up to oblige. Walk into Pottery Barn and you can buy not just a tablescape but an identity in one fell swoop: from Autumn Bright to Cutesy Country. My favourite is ABC Home, a warehouse full of a smörgåsbord of interiors sourced from India, Mexico and beyond. Every piece feels so unique, it's impossible to leave without buying something.

Our trip is also a chance to check out New York's department stores, our real competition. The Americans know how to put on a number; their stores are a mini universe of glamour and drama. Barneys, Bergdorf Goodman, Neiman Marcus, Henri Bendel: entering those luxury stores on Fifth Avenue made me feel as if I was in the heartbeat of American culture. They were simultaneously modern and grand – places where you could live a little larger, be in another zone, dream of a life you could have. In short, they epitomised aspiration.

Every floor had sales assistants who were knowledgeable and upbeat. 'Good morning, ma'am,' they'd greet you, almost unnervingly for those of us more used to the studied nonchalance or outright grumpiness of British shop assistants. In America they understood that the art of selling was about seduction, connection, warmth and service. And the sales associates' cheeriness was part of that. I loved the way department heads would hand you a personalised business card as you walked away, promising to send anything you needed direct to your hotel room. They might have been faking their enthusiasm, but Americans saw sales as a career. Not something that was beneath them.

It was the department store display budgets that really wowed me though. They knocked the socks off anyone else in the world. My contemporary at Barneys, British-born Simon Doonan, had half of the entire display team's budget to spend on windows alone. His work was extraordinary – and often as controversial as the artists before him. He'd done windows featuring coyotes stealing babies, installed chipped urinals and ratty sinks to counter the flounce of Yohji Yamamoto's menswear. His latest, which had really kicked up a stink, saw women being sawn in half and speared with knives. *The New York Times* had reports of people complaining it portrayed violence against women. Simon had to come out to reassure punters the windows were merely circus-themed.

I meet Callum at Dean & DeLuca in SoHo – the first place I'd seen turn a grocery store into a hip new hangout. We're sitting on high stools at the stainless-steel espresso bar, surrounded by apples with such a sheen they almost look fake. My head is sore after a big night out with Simon, but the sunny, crisp morning air of this great city perks me up. It's the kind of day where the steam from the subway grates hisses and swirls around your feet.

We start at Calvin Klein. At their Upper East Side offices, we're greeted by blonde Ivy Leaguers with French manicures and orthodontist-approved teeth. 'Welcome to Calvin. So great to see yoooooooou,' one enthuses, her drawl lasting so long I'm amazed she doesn't run out of breath. She breaks off only to inspect my Calvin Klein attire; the etiquette is that you wear the clothes of the designer brand you're meeting, so I'd had to pay for extra baggage allowance. Calvin has just launched his 'minimalist home collection', which was essentially a collection of white plates, white napkins and bed linen – also white. It might have been simple, but the way it was styled – graphically, with such a precise sense of space and place – was beautiful. 'So fresh,' I venture walking around the showroom, quickly running out of synonyms for the all-white attire. 'Lovely and clean.'

Ralph Lauren's aesthetic is a different game. He's taken that posh, shabby chic look so many Brits will recognise but removed any of the snootiness from it. He's ditched the dusty floral prints and the chintz, refined it into a new kind of old money look. Callum and I are convinced the Harvey Nichols women will love it. Stately and cosy. It's perfect for their country homes. If Callum can persuade the Ralph team to let us stock the collection in the UK.

The room set in his office – the Ralph Lauren showroom where they set up the collection as they'd want it to be displayed in a department store – feels like one of those rich aspirational homes you see in films: all equestrian, outdoorsy and rich. Weathered vintage leather armchairs, draped with cashmere plaid throws. Black-and-white photography, in thick white wooden frames, grouped with studied casualness on the wall. We're told Ralph has a strict brief for anyone wanting to stock his homeware: he refers to his in-store team as 'consultants', their job 'to guide you through the looks'. So when we found ourselves being talked through the Christmas collection by two consultants– all burgundy

112

velvet cushions and heavy cut-crystal tumblers – we knew we'd got the contract. What struck me most was how they really respected the product. They believed in it. And their belief was contagious.

That's the thing about New York. It radiates possibility. Looking up at the sliver of sky above huge skyscrapers, you feel both physically small and full of energy. Growth. Expansion. It's all around you.

While we're Stateside, Antonia also wants us to shore up relationships with our key fashion clients, so we head to Donna Karan's office in the Bronx. (She says she likes the grittiness of the area, but I imagine it's more about cheap rents. For all the smoke and mirrors, even the most buoyant fashion businesses are still run on a tight margin.) The journey at least gives me time to wrestle into Donna Karan's famous Bodysuit in the back of our yellow cab. The poppers are a bloody nightmare, but they're worth it. Donna Karan knows how to make clothes that make you feel sleek but still sexy. The Harvey Nichols customer has fallen hard for her 'Seven Easy Pieces' – the building blocks Donna Karan says every woman needs in her wardrobe. 'It's simple, really,' she says, perched atop her marble desk, covered in black-and-white Peter Lindbergh photographs from her new campaign. 'Bodysuit, skirt, tailored jacket, dress, white shirt, something leather, something cashmere. That's all a woman needs.' We're there to try and persuade Donna to come to London and host an in-store styling event around this concept. But she's not that interested in chatting. Instead, she's snogging her husband, who's about to head off on a business trip. It's been going on a full minute, tongues writhing, as we fiddle with our water glasses not knowing where to look. I make a mental note that female empowerment takes many forms.

We're on the red eye back from New York and go straight into the office, where the team are desperate for a download. I describe Simon Doonan's windows. I tell them about the beauty of a city that feels so alive, so lived in. Unlike London, where luxury is segmented into a few choice postcodes, New York has a heady mix where rarefied fragrance boutiques will overlook basketball courts where local kids shoot hoops. It's a juxtaposition I think we can learn from. Des wolf-whistles when I recall Donna Karan's snog. Until I tell him that she's agreed to do an in-store event with us next month – and I'm putting him in charge of showing her around.

In-store events are what it's all about right now. Some generate press coverage for Harvey Nichols, others get key customers into the store to spend on exclusive pieces Antonia and her team have acquired. But most are there to shore up the finances. Callum can push up the price of a concession by adding on an event. And he does. There's at least one a week, these days – more around peak seasons like Christmas.

The events are bringing in the cash for sure, but they're causing me and my team a headache. Earlier that year, I'd expanded my role to take charge of the publicity and marketing department. It had been something of a land grab. I'd heard that Suzy, who'd headed up the department, had decided not to come back after maternity leave. Her temp cover Camilla – a posh blonde who could run up a record expense claim but couldn't run a team – was hopeless, so I'd seen an opportunity. I wanted progress. A chance to prove myself. And I also knew that visual merchandising was never going to get me a seat on the board: for that I needed to run a department that delivered value to the business Ken couldn't argue was tangential. 'Offering editors free blow-dries and putting quarter-page adverts in the *Telegraph* isn't a financially prudent way to get customers on the shop floor,' I'd argued to Ken, knowing enough about the MD to centre my pitch to take over her remit around cold, hard numbers. That's also why I volunteered to do the first three months on my existing salary. I laughed off my ambition: 'You're getting a bargain.'

It was a punchy move; after all, I had no formal marketing qualifications. But, more valuable than letters on a diploma, I believed that if we wanted the world to write about us, we had to give them real stories. I wanted to work and collaborate with some of the most exciting stuff happening in London: artists, filmmakers, musicians, writers, poets – not just put on more mid-morning catwalk shows for wealthy women sitting there absently toying with their silk scarves and diamond bracelets. Bored women treating us merely as entertainment to pass their endless, empty days. If the windows were working to get Harvey Nichols talked about, we could do the same with events – centring them around anarchic ideas.

But before Donna Karan's visit to Harvey Nichols, we have several more low-key events to put together. Callum has promised burgeoning interiors brand Jerry's Home Store a flashy party to launch their concession on the fourth floor. It's up to us to deliver it. The only problem? It isn't exactly a household name.

Designed around the idea of a 50s American diner, Jerry's Home Store was a clever mix of statement zinc-topped tables and padded leather recliners, plus entry-level accessories like faux-vintage Coca-Cola glasses and ice-cream sundae kits for those who wanted to dip their toe into the trend. Ironically, it wasn't actually an American company. The Eton and Oxford-educated founder, Jeremy Sacher, couldn't have been more of an Englishman. But, as the great-grandson of Marks & Spencer's Michael Marks, he had retail in his blood, and had made a smart bet on Brits lapping up this unique brand of kitsch Americana.

'I've got a really good feeling about this,' Callum said, perhaps as much to hype himself up as anything else. He'd promised Jeremy Sacher a 500-square-foot premium pop-up space right where the escalators came up into the homeware department, plus a window and a launch party.

I've put Rita Brewer, my best PR manager, in charge of the Jerry's Home Store account. Furiously efficient, she's the grown-up of the group. Rita is only in her early thirties, but, as a no-nonsense mother of two young children who married the boy she grew up with in Bournemouth, she knows how to keep us all in check. She studied fashion design and started helping Katharine Hamnett with publicity alongside pattern cutting before realising that was her strength and moving into PR full-time. She loves work, often telling us that the world of luxury is a welcome counter to the chaos of snotty kids and nursery-school runs. But she also has no time for pretence, and thinks most designers are egotistical pains in the arse, the fashion press a snotty bunch of posh girls. 'Blimey, my mum wouldn't get this world,' she would often say.

Which is why I thought she'd be well placed to work with Jeremy Sacher and his wife Ros, who's taken on the role of PR officer for Jerry's Home Store. Ros is busy remerchandising the popcorn machines next to the ceramic bowls, decorated with pen portraits of the New York skyline. 'For Blockbuster home movie nights! Cheaper than the Odeon . . .' she laughs.

'That's the thing about husband-and-wife business owners,' Rita whispers to me. 'It's literally their lives.'

Set-up complete, Jeremy and Ros stand at the entrance, sipping on the strawberry milkshakes we've bought in for the launch instead of our usual fizz. They're watching the escalator, waiting for guests to arrive. Five minutes go by. Ten. Fifteen. The fashion press is notoriously always late, but this is veering into bum-clenching territory. Perhaps we've overdone it on the launches recently? We can't expect journalists to be in Harvey Nichols every night.

'Let me check on the canapés,' Rita says, retreating to the back of the space, out of earshot. She unclips her walkie-talkie. 'Guys, we need back-up,' she radios down to the press office. 'Get a handbag, get a notebook and get down here. I don't care what magazine you say you're from, but you love 50s Formica.'

Crisis over. But one thing was clear: I was going to have to rethink our publicity and marketing strategy.

Don't mess with Miss Muir

I'VE HAD MY FAIR SHARE of intimidating moments, meeting the grandes dames of the fashion world who wear judgement as naturally as black. The esteemed dressmaker Jean Muir was the scariest of all. Not because she was a diva, but because she was the real deal. Professional, exacting, in control. Over the last four decades, she established herself as the master of modern elegance: creating clothes that epitomised quiet luxury.

Antonia asks me to meet Muir. She says it's because she wants me to better understand one of the most important designers for our customers. The Harvey Nichols woman, she reminds me, has grown up buying Jean Muir's annual sewing patterns for *Vogue* and running up their own version of her dresses at home on their Singer sewing machine. Now they can afford to buy the original, not make the imitation, coming in for one of her immaculately cut wool gowns that'll work for a function at one of those swirly-carpeted hotels on Park Lane. They're chic but safe. A Jean Muir dress won't let you down, but it also won't outshine you.

For all Antonia's explanations, I hazard a guess that this meeting is as much a chance for her to demonstrate her power as a broker between me and designer. But whatever the reasoning, Antonia told me Miss Muir would see me at 2 p.m.

As I hurry back from lunch, I see Miss Muir waiting like Muriel Spark's Miss Jean Brodie. Dressed in a simple navy dress with a chopped-off bob and pale white make-up with purple lipstick that makes her look ghostly, she sits with legs crossed at the ankle, hands clasped in her lap. Her posture alone is enough to scare me off.

Over fresh mint tea, she speaks very slowly and precisely about how she envisages the window Antonia has promised her. 'I was thinking maybe the backdrop would be monochrome, hphrm,' she says, ending each sentence with a tic that sounds like a cat's mewling. I'm not sure whether to acknowledge it. Every so often, she'll break off mid-sentence with a beatific smile. I'm aware it isn't because she's happy. It's a sign that you are supposed to agree with what she's just said. 'Maybe Bridget could help do that?'

'Bridget?' I ask.

'Bridget Riley,' she replies, casually name-dropping one of the greatest living artists of the day. Of course they're friends.

Everyone who's anyone is in Miss Muir's gang. And if you want to make it in fashion, you'd do well to realise that – and find a way in too.

The creative art of management when you're dealing with loonies

IT's APPRAISAL SEASON AND, FOR once, I'm feeling confident. Callum has suggested we do mine over lunch at Bibendum. I should have known it wasn't because he thought I deserved a slap-up meal, but more because he couldn't be arsed to fill in the paperwork we've been sent by personnel. Callum's style was to work in the laziest way possible to get the most done. But he does care about the team he's built, and I respect his opinion.

'Mary,' he says. 'You're an absolute breath of fresh air in this old emporium and there's no doubt you have talent, drive and enthusiasm.' Then comes the tell-tale pause that means something else is on its way. 'However, with that enthusiasm comes an intensity and sometimes a lack of professional appropriateness. Telling your old deputy he should go and work for an average bag of crap retailer like Debenhams, where he would be seen as a genius with the second-rate ideas he showed you, is not only unkind but could land you into accusations of bullying. And I know you're not a bully, but there have been a few bits of feedback that suggest things can get a bit heated in your department. So I'm going to send you on some management training courses to double down on your strengths and guide you to becoming a charismatic, clever leader. Which I know you can be.'

He pops a seared scallop in his mouth and smiles. 'And anyway, there's nothing wrong with Debenhams. It's done some good numbers this month.'

'Yes,' I shoot back. 'But that doesn't mean it's loved. Or beautiful. Or a place where people want to hang out. That's what Harvey Nichols deserves to be. Not just a profit-making machine, but somewhere that means something to the people who shop here. Somewhere that excites and inspires people.'

I could feel myself losing control. I still hadn't learnt how to convey my point with Callum's composure and ease. He was a master of clarity and tact.

'Why can't a department store be more than selling beautiful stuff? Shouldn't we be trying to make it a space that is bigger than the designers and the product? I would bloody love Harvey Nichols to become *the* store that everyone talks about and wants to be a part of.'

He looks at me with a bemused smile. 'And I think you will, Ms Portas. I have absolutely no doubt about that. But you've got to learn to bring others on the journey.'

I know I can be easily frustrated by those around me not matching my speed or standards, but to hear it put so bluntly stings. I wonder whether someone has complained about me. I know personnel do tedious exit interviews with people who leave, but I'd always assumed that was a tick-box exercise to pop in a manila folder and close the drawer of the filing cabinet on, never to be seen again. It's true that I'm demanding of my team, that the pace is relentless. There's little time for reflection or pause; we're always onto the next thing. Oh God. I really feel thrown by this. I keep questioning myself, maybe I am a crap boss. I know I'm fiery, impatient and driven, but I really love my team and care about them.

The other day I'd found Rita sobbing in the fashion cupboard. She'd been humiliated by the matriarchal store manager Olive Oyl on the shop floor. Her crime? Not putting the execs' names in the correct order of seniority on the memo she'd printed out thirty-five times to stick into their individual pigeon holes. Rita was tough. So I knew it wasn't just a telling-off that had broken her; rather, it was months of operating under an increasingly intolerable pressure.

I felt that pressure too. Sometimes, I dreaded board meetings. The spotlight would land on your department, and you could be questioned on any part of your work, budgets, analysis, performance. All I could do was hope for a smooth ride. Most weeks, I wanted to go first just to get it over with – there was nothing worse than sitting through every other director's report, watching the clock tick down, knowing that, sooner or later, Ken would turn his glare on you. My God, the fear that used to shoot through me in those moments. Some weeks, it was fine. Other times, it felt like I was walking a tightrope, one wrong step away from disaster. My position was even more perilous. Unlike the others,

I wasn't a director. As a mere head of department, I knew I was more easily disposable.

Still, Callum's words stay with me. Later that week, I see Bean pull out her Tupperware. She's brought in devilled eggs again for lunch. The curried egg smell seeps through our corridor.

'Bean, can I take you out for lunch today?' I call out to her. 'It's so nice out there it seems a shame not to see any daylight.'

She flushes and throws some paperwork to disguise her packed lunch. 'That'd be lovely. Shall I telephone Signor Sassi and book us a table?'

The cosy Italian restaurant hidden off Knightsbridge may as well be the Harvey Nichols canteen. With palm trees everywhere, yellow napkins poking out of wine glasses and platters of pasta cooked to retain some bite, Signor Sassi feels like you've stepped into Milan for a moment. I love it there.

'I know I should have the branzino,' Bean says, scanning the menu. 'But my diet is actually going really well. I've lost seven pounds in two weeks doing SlimFast. So maybe one risotto alla Milanese won't hurt?'

I've learnt by now that Bean's always on a diet. Just as she's always in a tangle about a boy. This time, she tells me, it's about a Falklands-decorated veteran she's started dating. He has a flat in Notting Hill and a country pile in Norfolk. 'Ma and Pa think he's wonderful, of course,' she explains. 'And in many ways, he is. But I can see he's traumatised by whatever he saw out there. He shuts down easily and, you know me, I need someone who'll talk. I'm a sharer. An over-sharer, as my ma would say,' she laughs.

I'm not sure Bean is an over-sharer, but she has got an extraordinary empathy, a warmth — attributes, I remind her, she deserves to have recognised by a future partner. I'm probably the one overstepping, but this is what I adore about Bean. She is one part absolutely fucking useless as a secretary, and one part emotionally and intellectually alive. I often think that she's ended up in the wrong job. Like so many people, she's fallen into something she, or more likely her parents, thought she 'should' be doing. Her ability to analyse the behaviour of others would have made her a great therapist. She's made up for the many late nights I've spent sorting out her misfiled paperwork with long lunches like these, where she'll dive into existentialism or muse over whether Antonia is living an authentic life. (Hint: Bean thinks not.) I love these moments. And so does she.

I suddenly remember a gem Bean told me once. 'The thing I've always admired about you is that you can talk to the CEO or the cleaner. And there aren't many people who can — or will — do both.' Perhaps I need to realise that duality is my strength.

The egg whites

I CAN'T DO BREAKFAST MEETINGS any more. There's no breakfast. An egg-white omelette is the only thing anyone orders. Coming in at fifty-two calories out of the seventy in an average size egg, the yolk is too dangerous to pass through one's lips.

I know why they do it. They want to wear Azzedine Alaïa. And while *Vogue* might write that the designer's elasticated knit dresses suck you in so work for every shape, we all know that's bullshit. He's not called 'The King of Cling' for no reason.

I once heard of a fashion editor on a national newspaper buying an Alaïa high-waisted skirt that was so tight she couldn't sit down. 'No matter,' she apparently said. 'I'll just wear it to dînatoires.' The French word for dinner is all the rage on invites right now. Only it doesn't mean dinner; more a few canapés designed to take no more than two bites to eat and lots of vodka, lime and soda.

Still, the fashion editors I'm non-breakfasting with this morning don't go to sample sales. They don't even really need to buy clothes. Instead, they borrow samples direct from brands. As these

125

are the items designers make to show on catwalk models, they're minuscule. Anyone over a size 8 would be offered, whisper it, 'shop stock' – the items mere mortals buy full price from the shop floor.

Whether at fashion dinners in New York, Paris or London it pains me to see food ordered, cut up and moved around the plate, but then whisked away uneaten by the waiters. It's so wasteful. It's also wrong. Milan is the only city where it doesn't happen, where women's bodies still look like flesh, not skin and bones. Maybe it's baked into their heritage: the Rubenesque art you see hanging on the walls so often at the beautiful venues during Milan Fashion Week celebrate femininity. But here in London all the women around me seem to be starving themselves. Minimalising their sexuality. All for the sake of a bodycon dress.

Fashion is glamorous, artistic, innovative – and utter madness

To my friends and family, my life suddenly looks impossibly glamorous thanks to the places and people I'm interacting with in my role at Harvey Nichols. I'd joined a local theatre group – a nod to my RADA ambitions – and become friends with the women I acted alongside in Shakespeare comedies and Caryl Churchill plays. The crew would whoop when I turned up at one of our rowdy, bring-a-dish dinners, with grand platters of left-over food I'd scooped up after our press events. The egg whites won't have touched the caviar-topped blinis or salmon sashimi, but my people will dive in – their Delia Smith pork chops and chicken one-pots abandoned. These dinners restore me: in these moments, I felt a deep sense of belonging. It wasn't just about the plays we created but about the friendships we built, as I discovered that love has no age limit.

There was Dorrie, an eighty-year-old dynamo. Charonne, a mother of two teenagers, who also seemed to take me under her wing. Sharp as a tack and twice as funny, she could defuse the most stressful production crisis with a perfectly timed one-liner. But no one made me laugh like Kate.

Kate and I would take the piss out of each other mercilessly to the extent that rehearsals would have to stop while we bent over crying with laughter. When I arrived at the theatre late, carrying my latest Chanel bag or wearing some new Helmut Lang, Kate would purposefully grab an old wicker basket from the pile of props and spin around in her skirt, saying she'd bought it from the Sue Ryder designer charity shop.

But occasionally work and home would collide in the best possible way.

When the Royal Court Theatre gets in touch to see if Harvey Nichols will sponsor their latest performance, Emily Woof's *Revolver*, I know I want to make something happen. By now, I'm used to people approaching us to collaborate on projects, but I've been careful about who we work with. Partly it's about protecting the unique essence of Harvey Nichols, but it also riles me when marketing execs with big budgets think they can buy themselves credibility, courtesy of me and my plucky team. I want partnerships with people who share a vision, who can enhance and elevate the perception of Harvey Nichols while delivering new audiences. Even better when they bring two of my passions together. So I tell the Royal Court I'm not interested in simply putting Harvey Nichols' name in the programme and donating a wad of cash. If we're going to work together, it has to be more ambitious.

'Get me your top actors,' I propose, 'and I'll make a mannequin in their image and create a front run of windows. We'll get Britain's leading designers to make outfits for them and auction them off on opening night.'

By the next morning, John Gielgud, Harriet Walter and Alan Rickman are in.

'How wonderful,' says Antonia when I approach her about bringing the designers on board. I get the sense she's relieved to finally have me pitch a highbrow idea she can easily get behind. 'John might work with Paul Smith,' she muses. 'Something classic but complex. Nuanced. Like his performance of Prospero.' She's scribbling down thoughts, splotches of ink filling the page. Vivienne is perfect for Toyah Wilcox. All punk and performance.

'And then we can ask Betty and Jasper too, absolument.'

Alan Rickman comes in for a fitting. His droll performance as the villainous Sheriff of Nottingham opposite Kevin Costner in *Robin Hood: Prince of Thieves* has made him an unexpected heart-throb overnight, so I'm not surprised when Antonella brings him up to my office personally.

'Mary, meet Alan,' says Antonella smoothly. I'm constantly in awe of Antonella's relaxed confidence. She's got an extraordinary ability to make introductions as if she's dealing with guests at the village's cocktail party, not a global superstar. It's seamless. If only I can ignore the Double Ds peering in through the window, so close they may as well be snogging the glass.

I've asked comedian Ruby Wax if she'll host the auction for us, but the Royal Court thinks she's a controversial choice. Her new BBC comedy chat show has a reputation for making light of 'loonies' and IRA bombings. But she's hosted a few press events at Harvey Nichols over the last year and I have seen firsthand how she can really get the crowd going. I think her acerbic wit will shock the stuffy patrons, used to paying for little more than a gold plaque on the back of theatre seats, into spending big. Ruby agrees. 'As long as I can raid the shop floor for something to wear,' she barters. 'And sit me next to Alan Rickman at the dinner afterwards.'

The morning of the gala, I turn up at the theatre with my team to set up. Our plan is to have mannequins showcasing the designer outfits on stage behind Ruby Wax. But when I walk in, I see that Donald has improvised. He's spent weeks making papier-mâché masks that are supposed to resemble the actors we've worked with.

'I thought it would help get the bids up. Remind the audience of the star power behind the outfits,' he says proudly. The problem is that the actors' faces are horribly distorted. Gielgud looks like a frozen pea. Toyah resembles a rubber troll.

'Donald, you've got to get rid of them,' I tell him. 'I can see what you were trying to do, but this isn't working. They've got to go.'

We resort to printing masks of the real actors' faces, which we tape into the hands of the mannequins, positioning them so they cover the heads. Lemon-lipped Donald slinks off to have a fag; he's got the hump. But our remedy works, just about.

Front of house is thronging. We're in a world before celebrity publicists and roped-off VIP areas, so top editors, actors and wealthy patrons mingle freely. The British *Vogue* Editor-in-Chief

Liz Tilberis is making Judi Dench howl recounting how she punched a Parisian bouncer who wouldn't let her into the Jean Paul Gaultier show. Derek Jacobi and Emma Thompson are plotting what they're going to wear for the premiere of their new movie *Dead Again*. I'm in a corner with Kate who I've invited to be my guest, watching the event through her (gawping) eyes. The champagne and egos are the perfect mix for a heady atmosphere — one that gets only more riotous when we ask everyone to take their seats in the auditorium and deliver bottles of fizz to be passed down each row. It helps soften the blow when Ruby delivers her toxic takedown to kick off the auction.

I'm backstage giving an interview to Cathy McGowan for the new BBC One show *What's Going on in London* even though I know I've had too much to drink. Watching back my slightly slurred OTT performance on TV the next evening, I make a promise to myself to never drink at a work event again. But my hangover paranoia is eased by the fact that we've raised £17,000, a record for the Royal Court, and that trusting my instinct seems to be working. Now I just need to do it even more.

An audience with the Queen's dresser

'LET US HAVE LUNCHEON,' THE card says. It's perfect penmanship, written on thick cream card. Sir Hardy Amies is embossed in burgundy at the top.

I've been asked to meet the Queen's official dressmaker for poached salmon and new potatoes at Claridge's. He wants to discuss the Harvey Nichols glory days, when the cashmere came in shades that ranged only from milky tea to a builder's brew.

Antonia urged me to borrow a Max Mara camel coat for lunch. 'It's a classic,' she trilled, deploying the most overused word in fashion.

I'm not going to borrow something every forty-year-old seems to come in and buy like it's a fashionable rite of passage. I'm not interested in dressing the part. I know what suits me, what gives me confidence – a Helmut Lang suit.

I love this suit. It's what I wear when I don't have the headspace to think about what to wear. When I need something that'll work for the mad entirety that my days now encompass: a board meeting, lunch at Claridge's and a champagne-fuelled fashion party to finish.

The way Helmut Lang cuts tailoring just works for my height. It's nipped in at the waist, strong in the shoulder but with long, louche trousers. It's constructed but simple. And while I know Antonia will roll her eyes at my wearing trainers to lunch with the Queen's couturier, I always wear my box-fresh Keds with this suit. They keep it from feeling too formal.

'Darling, I really have to tell you,' Sir Hardy says, launching straight in as we sit down at the most discreet table in Claridge's. 'You really must stop doing those fucking godawful windows.'

Only one response comes to mind. 'I'll think about it, Sir Hardy – when you stop doing those fucking godawful dresses.'

There's silence. And then he laughs.

Money men with balls and bullshit
do really well

'IN THE MODERN WORLD THE stupid are cocksure, while the intelligent are full of doubt,' the philosopher Bertrand Russell wrote. I'm reminded of his words so often these days.

Retail is a brutal business. A department store is only as good as its sales per square foot of the shop floor. Every year, Ken will identify the poorest performing 20% of our brands and give them twelve months' notice to improve sales or be booted out. That was often more time than he'd give his employees. I'd seen enough of my colleagues fired to know that there was no room for complacency. Many crumbled under the pressure. When Ken singled you or your department out, you went into every meeting expecting the so-called hairdryer treatment: a rant so fierce it'd feel like you were in a wind tunnel. But others, me included, thrived. The work was tough, but that made the rewards all the more satisfying.

I'd worked hard to get under the skin of the numbers, understanding that I couldn't afford to ignore them. When I'd first arrived at Harvey Nichols, I'd sought out the finance director, a wonderful, avuncular older man named Nigel. He knew I was a creative and that numbers and budget planning weren't high on my list of expertise. But he showed me. And he used to smile when I turned up for my quarterly budget review, often saying, 'Now, Mary – when I say budget, it's not a suggestion. It's what you must keep to.' Because I'd learnt from my mum to be meticulous with a weekly grocery budget, I would often actually come in under. Then he would smile and say, 'Spend it, Mary. It's yours. Otherwise Ken will take it and over the months you will find your annual budget decreasing.' I came to enjoy my meetings with him. He went on to teach me the bigger picture of the business. How the buying budget worked. What open to buy meant. What capex meant. How the store design budget worked differently from my display one. I realised that I wasn't stupid at finance. In fact, I was good, and he loved being my teacher.

But eventually Ken decided we needed to get more efficient, and what better way than bringing in one of the big financial consultancy firms to scrutinise every department's spending, our margins and overall profitability? I remember the morning after the announcement, heading down to see Nigel, only to find him chatting to a man he introduced as Seb Davey.

He sat there like he owned the air in the room, legs spread just enough to make a point, one arm draped over the back of the chair, the other resting easy on his knee. That effortless, sprawling confidence – the kind that says, *I'm comfortable, and you should be uncomfortable* – radiated off him. Not slouched, not stiff, just perfectly poised in that way certain men seem to master, like they've spent years perfecting the art of looking like they don't care while making sure everyone notices them.

Seb made out he had walked away from the City and its fat bonuses back when the Square Mile had more cocaine than money going through it. 'The wife wanted babies, and I thought, yup, goodbye, good times, slow the pace down and enter the world of luxury.' Now, here he was, working for a consultancy, stepping into our world to show us all how to squeeze out every last efficiency, whether we liked it or not.

I avoided interactions with him by being ruthless about my budgets, finding increasingly madcap ways to hit the bottom line without sacrificing the end result. 'Ralph Lauren wants a window? Of course, but it'll cost five grand, minimum. You can't find a realistic replica horse for less. And Ralph really does expect the show ponies,' I'd rationalise. The excess budget went on windows we actually wanted to deliver: an upside-down living room, tables and chairs welded to the ceiling, Alice in Wonderland style, to launch the latest homeware collection. Now that really was expensive. Even before health and safety.

When we actually did run out of cash, with a month to go before year-end, I panicked. Then called Lucia van der Post, founding editor of the *Financial Times' How to Spend It* magazine, aka the Grande Dame of Luxury.

'I don't suppose you've got a few copies of old newspapers hanging around, have you?' I asked. 'Well, more than a few. Enough to cover twenty-seven windows?'

When she liked you, Lucia was a woman who got things done. A week later, 185 bundles of old *Financial Times* arrive in the loading bay. I wanted to create a seascape through the window by folding and stacking hundreds and hundreds of newspapers and sculpturally placing them as waves rising as high as ten feet down to the floor and splashing against the glass. 'Then we'll dress the mannequins in the slickest trouser suits,' I riff. 'We'll make out it's a statement on corporate chic.'

The *FT* wants to write about it and the collection in the following weekend's edition; the team, however, wants to kill me. Cass has spent all day stacking, folding and trimming thousands of newspapers before precariously wiring the mannequins into place. As she shuts the window door, we all hear the crash of a mannequin head butting the glass. It must have slid down the tsunami of papers. 'Fuuuuuccck,' we shout in unison.

Donald comes running from the side windows he's been in charge of. He's high on glue after plastering pages to windows. He'd tried to make sure the story of Nelson Mandela's election to President of the ANC was front and centre of window 12, but Des had covered it with Richard Gere and Cindy Crawford at the Oscars. 'Phwoar. That Versace number is almost enough to turn me,' he'd joked of Cindy's plunging red gown.

While we obsess over every penny, the Harvey Nichols customer isn't holding back. Fashion is booming. Designers are now household names: Versace, Calvin and Ralph as rich as the clients who clamour over the labels, logos and luxury taking over the shop floor.

I can see why this is happening. Catwalk shows have gone from salons in designer showrooms, with rich clientele sitting on antique gold chairs as models waft around, to blockbuster performances about to be beamed around the world on Fashion TV.

There's a nervous energy before a catwalk show from one of the great storytellers like John Galliano, now at Dior, or Franco Moschino. You never know what to expect. I remember one Moschino show where Franco himself sat front row to watch dresses made of plastic bin bags come down the catwalk before rising suddenly and shooing them off stage. He later said it was a commentary on the fashion industry's tendency to remake, reinterpret rather than invent.

So you always feel a sense of anticipation in the crowd before a show as they surge into the space – a customary ten minutes late – clamouring to see how it's staged. Draped with satin curtains or bright white, lighting so flashy everyone keeps their sunglasses on, Galliano uses every trick in the book to create a mood before you've even seen an item of clothing. The chatter of guests positioned in rows that denote their status comes to a natural hush when the music blares out: a sign the show is about to start. While *Vogue*'s fashion critic Sarah Mower will scribble in her notebook, drawing lines of shapes, writing single words that stand out – 'chartreuse' or 'joyful' – for me it's more a sum of parts. The stage, the lights, the music, the models, the movement and, yes, the clothes, it's a piece of performance art. Sometimes, like the best plays, it's only afterwards, days later, when you're still thinking about the shape or the mood, the impact of the show really sinks in.

No one creates impact quite like Gianni Versace, though. Who with one catwalk show has proven that Fashion Week is about so much more than selling clothes to buyers and press – it's entertainment. Sending Cindy Crawford, Christy Turlington, Linda Evangelista and Naomi Campbell down his black mirrored catwalk lip-synching to George Michael's 'Freedom!' was the kind of move marketeers dream of. Apparently, he'd paid them $15,000 each, but it worked. Even my local newsagent was desperate to talk to me about it when I went in there to pick up the new *Vogue* – and get the scoop on the supermodels who were now global superstars. 'Linda is a goddess,' I was happy to report.

As fashion established itself as entertainment, so our strategy for windows that got people talking made more sense – and took on more currency. We pushed the themes; no idea was too outlandish. And customers lapped it up. Probably because they had moved on too.

We've gone from Fiona in Fulham in her frilly blouses to a woman who knows her own mind and has her own cash. She's buying Versace's skintight catsuits or over-the-knee patent boots worn with flippy-hemmed miniskirts. We can't keep Moschino Cheap and Chic in stock. Three-figure handbags designed to look like brown paper bags with leather baguette loaves poking out of the top are flying off the shelves. Those who can't afford them opt for the jewellery – gold, bold and flashy. Meanwhile, Dolce & Gabbana's reinvention of La Dolce Vita is winning over customers desperate to get their hands on the Italians' taffeta wraps draped over velvet corsets or jewelled bra tops at £2,000 a pop. 'I mean, who's paying £200 per paste gem?' Rita would scorn. Her mum had raised her to believe the right aesthetic could change a woman's fortunes. She didn't think Versace's was it.

Survival

ONE MONDAY MORNING, FRESH BACK from annual leave, one of my design team appears in my office asking Bean if he can see me. He's come to tell me he's decided to do something he'd been thinking about for a while: quit. When I ask what department store he's jumping ship to, the answer stuns me into a rare silence. He's leaving without a job to go to. We're similar ages, and I know the job market is buoyant right now, but clearly we operate in different worlds. I could never imagine having the luxury of resigning without a job to go to. The jump to Harvey Nichols means I'm now earning the same as Graham, but I don't think I'll ever feel financially secure. Mind you, there are some virtues in staying put when you really want to just say fuck it, I'm off. It's taught me resilience: a staying power, if you like.

Unlike so many of the people around me who'd dreamt hard and worked harder to get into their roles, I'd fallen into this world almost by accident. But I'd always given it my all. I liked my reputation as the person you could rely on, the one who made things happen. It was partly because I didn't want to let myself down. And partly control – because I couldn't.

When you have had nothing – not just no money, but no home, no parents; when you're an orphan (even though I hate that word because I can't bear the pity and image it conjures of a small, lonely figure in tattered clothes) – it's impossible not to fear returning to that place. That sense of self-preservation runs deep. I know that I have to look after myself because nobody else is going to. I'm not bitter about that; it's just a fundamental truth I've come to accept.

But it gave me a strong creative drive: an ambition to not just preserve life, but to be alive, to feel alive. I need security, but I constantly crave self-fulfilment, excitement and newness – a desire to create, build and move forward.

Sometimes I feel guilty my job is so all-consuming, but the thought of not doing this never enters my mind. When Kate occasionally berates me for having my head still half in Harvey Nichols land when she's trying to talk to me about life, I'm contrite but also bemused. Work–life balance doesn't exist for me. I'll think of ideas in the shower, I'll run through paperwork on the train. I'm consumed by work but because it excites me, keeps my brain fizzing. Besides the fun, or perhaps because it is so fun, is a near-constant fear of being fired. A fear that, I'm ashamed to admit, so often stops me from freely being me or speaking out when I see behaviour that makes me and my team feel shit. Sobbing in the fashion cupboard's become so commonplace, the juniors have their own code. When the Beastie Boys is blasting out from the stereo, you don't disturb them. You constantly hear rumours that one of the senior management team is shagging his secretary, but short of offering her first dibs at the office beauty sale and thinking 'Christ, she'd better be careful,' this behaviour largely goes uncommented on. In fact, if I'm truly honest, I didn't see how utterly crap this was. I took it for granted.

Sometimes the most obvious, important realities are the ones that are hardest to see and talk about. And there was no discussion about 'workplace culture'. You were there to work and to succeed. You accepted the ways things were, that your bosses would swear at you. You accepted that there was sexual harassment and innuendo. Bullying. Humiliation. A sense you had to diminish yourself in some parts and extend yourself in other ways to fit in.

My pal, a really gentle guy who ran the display department at another store, once told me about a conversation he had with his boss. He went in, laid it out plainly: *Look, I know you've cut the budgets, and I understand, but I'm really struggling to deliver the same level of creative work with what's left.* He wasn't complaining, just being honest. The response? No discussion, no sympathy, just four blunt letters: JFDI. A new acronym for me at the time: *Just Fucking Do It.*

The constant vigilance, the pressure to succeed, the awareness that it could be you packing up your desk one Friday was intense. It crushed some people, who left as shells of their former selves. But it was nothing like the rumours emerging from our neighbours down the road in Harrods. Everyone whispered about the way pretty, young shop-floor girls would check their bags before they left for the day. They'd heard tales from others who'd had Crème

143

de la Mer moisturiser and Judith Leiber crystal clutches planted in their belongings. When they were picked up by burly security placed on the back door, their only route out of being written off as a thief was to have a private audience with Mr Al Fayed.

Harvey Nichols, like any alpha culture, was a workplace geared around winning, but that worked well for me. For all the toughness, I loved and thrived working in a dynamic, high-performance team with a laser focus on results. And a lot of craziness and laughter along the way. Still, I'd decided that, if I was in an environment where status and salaries mattered, then I was going to play this game and be properly recognised for the work I was doing.

I wanted to get promoted. And, given the buzz I'd brought to the store, I knew I deserved a place on the board.

Earlier that year, I'd been put forward for a directorship. But in a tactic that was classic Antonia, she'd let it slip that my promotion had been scuppered in the board meeting by Callum and I'd been given a token pay rise instead. 'Ma chérie, I'm sorry,' she cooed, seeing my devastation. 'I thought you knew.'

Callum had always been a supporter. His freedom and light-touch management had been good for me – allowing me the creativity I craved. But I was under no illusion: he gave me autonomy because he knew what I created helped him too. I was good at making him look good. And now, in my heart, I knew he wanted to maintain that dynamic. He didn't want me to be the same level as him. I challenged him on it, and he told me honestly that he thought I needed another year. And so I had to wait.

In bed with Ralph Lauren

RALPH LAUREN'S TEAM HAVE SENT through his instructions for the Christmas installation space he's taking in the homeware department. It runs to three pages. Double-sided.

I start reading out some of the bullet points to Rita. 'European pillows must be arranged at a forty-five-degree angle to the king or queen. Only one bolster per arrangement . . .' You need a maths PhD to get this right.

But get it right, we must. Because Ralph himself is coming over to open the space. It's a coup to get the main man over for an event in the store, but Ralph Lauren Home is – as Callum predicted – selling brilliantly. The audience is lapping up his all-American look, and Antonella says that the demand from her VIP customers for a private meet-or-greet with the designer has been off the scale. 'He's the Father Christmas of the Home Counties,' she jokes.

Ralph is staying at the Hyde Park Hotel, across the road from the store in his usual suite, but has sent his minions to oversee the set-up. A small army of American women are packed into the square space, all eager to demonstrate that they know Ralph's wishes best. The fact that they look identical – blue jeans, white shirt, navy jacket, with a blowout that would have kept Greta's Vincenzo tied up all morning – makes it even harder to keep up.

'This is how Ralph likes his glasses,' one drawls, moving the glassware into groups of threes: water, wine and champagne. Coupes, never flutes.

'Ralph really likes the way the velvet burgundy sings against the brown,' another purrs, rearranging the pillows for the fifteenth time.

'This bed needs remaking. Ralph will want the corners sharper,' a third says, ripping apart the bedding. They might be acting like they're on first-name terms with him, but it's clear they're also used to being told off by a man who has built his business on a very specific aesthetic.

'OK, we're all set. Great job,' his assistant chirrups with a false optimism. 'We'll telephone ahead when he leaves the hotel so you can get ready.' Ralph requires a receiving line of sorts.

I'm working late that night when I decide to triple-check the space. It's not a chore. I love wandering through the department store late at night while it's quiet, lit only by the streetlights that seep through the windows creating a host of unusual shadows on the shop floor. As I near the Ralph space, I see a Hoover discarded on the cranberry shag-pile rug. Surely Rita's team wouldn't have been sloppy enough to leave it when they were setting up? Then I notice the bed is rocking – two of the cleaners are under the covers going at it like the clappers. Those sheets have got a 400-thread count. Thank God they're not white.

It's a fine line between fabulous and failure

I HEAR LYNNE FRANKS BEFORE I see her. She's sitting, cross-legged, her paisley kaftan carpeting the kitchen floor, chanting. 'Ommmmmm . . .' she bellows. I swallow down my scepticism. However bizarre this New Age scene seems, I'm in the home of London's best-connected woman. Which means, before long, we'll probably be selling the marble Buddhas that surround her at Harvey Nichols.

The premier PR mogul, Lynne handles the publicity for everyone from the Pet Shop Boys to Tommy Hilfiger. A connector, a networker, she turns up to every event and has no shame in asking a favour or suggesting a new business idea – even if you didn't ask her for it. There are some in the industry who roll their eyes at Lynne's relentless adoption of the Next New Thing, whether or not it suits her far from sample-size body or whitewashed, million-pound Maida Vale home. But ultimately, fashion is an egos game, so most are won over by the way Lynne fangirls over them, committing in entirety to everything from colonics to catsuits.

Lynne shouldn't really be talking to me. She'd been on contract to do the PR for Harvey Nichols for years. But when I'd taken over the publicity team, I'd decided to end the contract. I didn't relish having difficult conversations like that, but I was getting better at them. I always did them first thing in the morning, otherwise I knew I'd spend the whole day obsessing over what was to come. And I tried to be as straight as I could. The other person might despise me, but at least I knew I'd done what I felt instinctively was right. So I explained to Lynne that severing her contract wasn't personal; rather, it was a way to claw back the budget. I felt the department needed to be able to pursue big ideas, and I wanted my team in-house to be made up of a mix of creatives, thinkers and writers. I wanted people who helped me create the stories, not just PR them. She'd cried. Then asked if she could keep her discount.

For a while, my rationale had worked. To mark London Fashion Week, I worked with a two-strong team of textile artists to bespoke the giant bearskin hats that they sourced from the same supplier as the Queen's Royal Guards. We styled all the mannequins in the best of the cool Brit designers – Galliano, Westwood – wearing these crazy headpieces. The public loved it. Even Elspeth was a fan. Leaving work late one night, I'd seen her take one of the damaged hats off the skip where we'd dismantled the window paraphernalia ready for a new set-up, striding off into the SW1 streets wearing it.

With the triumphs came parts of the role I found tough – endless events. A dinner to celebrate Louis Vuitton's Pochette bag hitting the shop floor . . . A party for the launch of Angel by Thierry Mugler, with its revolutionary star-shaped glass bottle . . . I found so much of organising these tiresome. As brilliant as my team were, event planning was all about the detail. We'd spend hours discussing what canapés were en vogue, how the napkins should be folded, who absolutely couldn't sit next to who. Big-picture vision was my drug; minute details bored me – and I knew they weren't my forte. Then, after hours of planning that I believed could have been spent more creatively, you'd still have the event to attend. Outfit choices, blow-dries . . . the physicality was exhausting enough without all the hours of small talk.

My team assumed my love of being on stage in my local theatre group meant I was a natural at a late-night party. But, for me, the theatre wasn't about just performing; it was all about the observation. 'Why is she behaving like that? What's making her speak that way? What makes her dress that way?' Questions I loved asking myself – and ones that, I believed, had helped me foster creativity and diverse perspectives and approaches to my work. By contrast, I found the constant showiness of events exhausting. Flailing, I knew I needed help from the best. Which is why I'd come to Lynne: the professional socialiser. Despite no longer having the PR contract, she agreed to help. Besides, I really liked her. She made me laugh and I admired her gumption. The way her madcap manoeuvring always resulted in something arresting.

We had to finesse a guest list for the store's new-season launch, as I tried not to gag over mushy lentils that smelled like old plant water. 'It's vegan. Annie Lennox gave me the recipe,' Lynne assures me, before launching into instructions. 'Put Jennifer on there too. Betty says she's working on a new sitcom about the fashion industry.' She means Jennifer Saunders, a comedian who is already hot property thanks to *French and Saunders*, a sketch show that is one of the BBC's biggest-budget series. Lynne doesn't know much more than that Saunders is looking for material to spoof and has found rich pickings in fashion. Knowing her work, it'll be cutting – and hilarious. I decide there and then Harvey Nichols must be part of it.

'Forget some ridiculously expensive billboard – if we get onto this show, we'll be in people's living rooms every Friday night,' I riff with Rita later. 'It's a risk, I know, but somehow it feels right.' We're discussing how to pitch Harvey Nichols being embedded in the sitcom: what we can offer them to make us integral to the story.

Comedy is where it's at right now: a bunch of anarchic kids have given the genre a momentum the tap-dancing duo Morecambe and Wise could never achieve. I've seen from watching Ruby Wax in action, that people – even the eye-rolling fashion crew – are drawn to this kind of cover-your-eyes comedy. There's a new freedom in the sense that anything goes. An edge I'm drawn to.

If Jennifer's new sketch show is even half of that, it'll be gold dust. I need to make sure we're part of it. Not least because I can't bear the thought of a competitor department store stealing that kind of exposure away from under us.

Multiple calls and faxes later, having made several introductions with the great and the good of the fashion world, Jennifer Saunders is sitting in my office. She looks just like the woman you see on TV, but aloof, with an inscrutable face. There's no sign of humour. She barely says a word. Increasingly bemused but bullish, I'm offering up full access to Harvey Nichols to break the silence.

'You can film after hours, inside and out. A free rein to borrow whatever designer clothes you want,' I say, only briefly wondering if I need to get this approved by the board.

'OK,' she replies laconically. 'Perhaps.'

I make a calculated guess that taking Jennifer onto the shop floor to see the customers in action might help. And it's true that she starts to perk up as we wander through the rails. She watches as two women coo over the new floral brocade Lacroix, scribbling notes furtively. She sweeps up orange pleated Issey Miyake and Gucci's newest bamboo-handled bags. 'Can I take some pictures of these?' she asks.

It's then that we run into Antonia, on her way back from the homeware department carrying a 20s Tiffany-style vintage lamp.

'Antonia, this is Jennifer Saunders,' I introduce them. 'Her next show is about fashion, so I'm giving her the tour.'

'Oh, marvellous. Hello, lovely to meet you,' Antonia says, awkwardly moving the lamp under her arm to shake hands. 'Honestly, I mean I love Holland Park, I really do. And if my current place had just 10% more light, 12%, I could call it the house pour toujours, but I just can't. Well, the art won't fade, I suppose . . .' she trails off, suddenly seeming to notice the pile of clothes Jennifer is holding. She frowns. 'I suppose bright colours work better on camera.'

152

Weeks later, Antonia corners me to ask what's going on. I know she feels I'm encroaching on her territory. 'Darling, you owe me the information. Remember, you might be the engine, but I'm the car,' she says.

In the end, it's the fact that Joanna Lumley will be Jennifer's co-star that convinces Antonia to get onboard. But by now I've spent so long convincing Antonia that securing Harvey Nichols a starring role in the BBC's show is a good idea, I've forgotten to ask myself whether it really is. It's one thing creating a window display that causes gridlock on Sloane Street. That only lasts six weeks. A primetime comedy that'll disrupt the store for months and that seven million people will tune into every Friday night is a very different kind of gamble. And I've still not been allowed to see the script. What if the store is the butt of the jokes? In my bullish haste, I realise I haven't considered this enough. All I know is it's called *Absolutely Fabulous*. Mind you, it's too late for second thoughts: the crew starts filming tomorrow.

I know that beneath me on Knightsbridge a thirty-strong crew are rigging up lights and cameras to film outside the store. I decide it can't hurt to check how it's going and creep down the back stairs and out into the perfume hall.

When a department store is silent at night, lights dimmed, it's like your senses attune. The familiar musky vanilla scent of Calvin Klein's Obsession still hangs in the air. Floodlights glare from the dark street through the double-fronted doors. All I can see is Joanna Lumley's blonde beehive illuminated in the glare. It's swaying, ghostlike, as she waves her arms around. It looks like she's a toddler writing her name in the night sky with a sparkler – only it's a glowing fag butt, not a firework.

What sounds like cackling breaks the silence on the shop floor. It's coming from one of the windows. 'Hello?' I call out.

'Maaaary! Let us out,' comes the voice of Des from the other side of the six-inch plywood that seals the window displays. I find the catch and hinge the door open to find Des and Donald slumped against our new mannequins, sweating profusely.

'What are you two doing in here? And what the fuck have you got on?' I cringe. Des's Versace leather trousers are so tight I have to avert my eyes from down there. Donald's Moschino cropped top isn't much better. The pair have clearly raided the fashion cupboard – and if Antonia finds out, we're all going to be in trouble.

'We just thought we'd pop in and change the light bulbs. Get ahead for tomorrow.' Des swallows. 'And then the crew said that if we were here, we'd have to stay put.'

'Something about the consistency of the shots,' continues Donald smoothly, as if they've had hours to work out their cover story. 'The security guards closed the door. Locked us in.' He puts his hand over his mouth and raises his eyebrows. 'Ever so naughty of us, aye,' he says coyly before we all get the giggles.

I laugh as Tweedledee and Tweedledum shuffle back upstairs with me, tripping up on the sample size nine shoes that definitely don't belong to them.

I've barely changed out of my commuter trainers the next morning, before Bean starts fussing. She still hasn't understood that the best skill a secretary can have is keeping us both calm. 'Ken wants to see you in his office,' she mumbles. 'He asked me to tell you to go there as soon as you got in.'

I'm briefly distracted by a memo on my desk from the Double Ds claiming overtime for last night's antics (the bloody cheek), but I know not to keep the MD waiting.

As I arrive at Ken's office, Antonia is just leaving. 'Bonjour, ma chérie,' she chirrups as she scurries away.

'I'll cut to the chase,' Ken starts. 'What you're going to find, Mary, with me . . . One, I don't like being out of the loop. Two, I don't like surprises. And three, I don't need any more trouble in my life. My wife gives me enough of that.' It's clear that Antonia has told him about the filming.

I do my best to explain that Jennifer Saunders is the reigning queen of British TV. To convince him that Harvey Nichols having a starring role in a BBC comedy show will take us to a new audience. That it's free marketing – he just has to trust me.

Reluctantly, he agrees. But not without a parting shot. 'But I can't see how comedy and luxury sit together. As long as this isn't sending up the store. I know British humour. All sarcasm and cynicism. The Chairman's over next month and I don't need any more grief.'

When I confront Antonia afterwards, she's the picture of child-like innocence. 'Oh, darling. He didn't know? I had no idea. Ma faute,' she faux-cries. 'But don't worry, I'm sure it'll be fine.'

She's fiddling with that crucifix again. And her jitteriness is contagious.

Chefs are the new rockstars

FILMING WRAPPED, WE'LL HAVE TO wait for months until *Absolutely Fabulous* airs. I try to put it out of my mind, to compartmentalise the anxiety and move on to more pressing matters. Meanwhile, in what they think is a clever pun, management has hired Harvey's – Marco Pierre White's buzzed-about restaurant – for the office summer party. It's miles away, but they know we'll all make the pilgrimage to Wandsworth for oyster tagliatelle cooked by the youngest chef to be awarded two Michelin stars. On the way to the loo, I spot the chef having a fag with his team. He looks me and my Donna Karan cold-shoulder dress up and down. 'Come. Sit. Have a drink with me,' he laughs, pulling up a chair, proving that in this new era of rock 'n' roll chefs, he's the lead singer.

Knocking out a cookbook that sells millions every six months, Delia Smith has got the nation hooked on food. But, just like so often happens, now it's evident that food can be big business, the men have moved in. It's a pattern. Suddenly restaurants helmed by superstar chefs are the new place to be seen – and the hippest are stealing our customer spend.

At the office party, talk soon turns to the plan to reinvent the Harvey Nichols restaurant. The prevailing wisdom has been that food and beverages are a waste of premium retail space. But the Chairman has seen retail and hospitality dovetailing successfully in the sky-high shopping malls across Asia and believes doing something similar here will make Harvey Nichols not just a shop but a destination. He has brought in a wave of sharp, food-savvy young men – charismatic, ambitious and clearly drawn to the momentum of this burgeoning industry to run the new department of food and beverages. Charles, Will and the other public schoolboys turned claret connoisseurs are sampling menus and stocking the wine cellar with New World gems. 'Nothing too fruity,' they sniff.

Meanwhile, our offices are being ripped out to build a new restaurant, champagne bar and food hall on the fifth floor, something no department store's ever thought to create.

We're basing the space on New York's Dean & DeLuca – all stainless steel, monochrome and sans serif type. We'll surround the bar with a food hall, with coffee beans we'll grind on site, silver canisters of tea you'll want to display on your shelf at home and hampers that'll become the new status gift. The restaurant will even have its own express elevator straight to fifth. Buzzy. Fast. Very Big Apple.

'We need something splashy for the launch,' Ken tells me. Everyone knows this is the Chairman's personal project – his first major move since buying Harvey Nichols. The refit has cost him a small fortune. In other words, it *has* to work.

I task a wonderful young artist, whose metal and bronze sculptures I had seen weaving through Manchester Piccadilly, to create a thirty-foot-long installation of a fish using recycled baked bean cans. I want the body of the fish open with shelves, so I can stuff it with the produce we'll be stocking: Harvey Nichols-branded packets of biscuits and cheese crackers, wine, jars of deli-style sundried tomatoes, paper packets of coffee beans, exotic teas. I'll get Jules to paint 'SEASonal Food Now Sold Here' in punchy lettering across the fish.

Cass and her crew spend weeks ripping their fingers to shreds to make mini versions for in-store, deconstructing the metal, hammering it flat and then warming it by blowtorching it to shape the smooth metal into the fish's gills.

'I thought I was here to sell fashion, not some poxy tins of poached sardines,' she moans, ripping open another pack of chocolate chip cookies intended for the installation. 'And I'm going to get fat with all this lying around.'

While the builders are putting the finishing touches to the fifth floor, we've been moved to a temporary office down the road. As we totter up Sloane Street carrying boxes stuffed to the gills with gills ready to be constructed, I run into Elspeth.

'Mary, what have you got there?' she calls out. I try to explain the concept of the food hall, but I can tell she's not interested.

'Listen, have ye gotten any more of those posho creams?' she interrupts. The team had been doing their seasonal clear-out of the samples knocking around in the beauty cupboard and we'd passed on a few bits to Elspeth. 'The good stuff. I don't want any of that cheap shit that I can get at any high street counter.' You can't fault her taste.

It takes us hours to string the installation into place, hole-punching and threading wire cord through and up onto the ceiling fixtures so the fish is secure but flexible. Ensuring it works as one big piece and looks like it's swimming through the six windows on Sloane Street.

'It's causing quite the stir,' the doorman tells me later that week. Harold is my barometer. Standing guard for weeks on end, he knows the rhythm of the customer better than all of us. When he says they like a window, it means they really do.

The customer might like watching the bright lights reflecting off the fish's shiny gills, but sadly it's not doing its job. The fifth floor is still really slow to take off. Only a few people sit at the circular, stainless-steel champagne bar. You can hear the cutlery clinking as staff set up tables in the empty skylit café. Devoid of customers, the fruit, meat and fish that's painstakingly arranged each morning lies there all day, untouched. Waxy Amalfi lemons with green stalks that look like they belong in a Vermeer still life are chucked away at the end of the week. Rita goes home with more pork chops than even her boys can eat. It's a disaster.

The month-end board meeting is even tenser than usual. You can tell Ken's stressed: he's adding sweetener to his coffee. 'We need ideas, folks. And fast,' he says, tapping his pen impatiently on the desk.

Over the upcoming months, we try everything. Stunts like selling 'supper in a paper bag' get us column inches. But while the press loves the idea of a modern, metropolitan woman who needs a curated edit of that night's ingredients right down to a single garlic clove, it doesn't bring the women themselves into store. We try collaborations with key tastemakers. Rita manages to persuade Cynthia Musgrave to shell out for a concession. The Cotswolds Sloane who's pivoted into flower arranging after stealing cuttings from Sudeley Castle to start her own rose garden is all the rage. But the glass-roofed, sun-drenched space is too hot: by 3 p.m., the flowers are wilting and so are we. The space is beautiful. It should be buzzing. But perhaps it's too radical, too ahead of its time. How long will it take for the customer to catch up?

'Oh, it's *Absolutely Fabulous* . . .'

A s HYPE AROUND *ABSOLUTELY FABULOUS* begins to build ahead of its November 1992 release date I start to worry. Now we're mortgaged up to the hilt, I can't afford to lose my job. Bean brings me a copy of the new *Radio Times*. Joanna and Jennifer, in a garish sequin bomber jacket and red tights, are on the cover. 'It's Lumley and Saunders keeping up with the trendies,' reads the coverline introducing BBC Two's new comedy. 'Do you think we might be in the background shots?' Bean asks gleefully. The feature inside talks about how Ruby Wax had been working with Saunders on the script – and that it's set to poke fun at an industry that's not known for its sense of humour. I feel sick reading that. Is Harvey Nichols about to get skewered?

At school, I was always the one taking it that one step too far. I'd often have to take the phone at home off the hook so that the Catholic nuns who ran the school couldn't call to report my antics to Mum. Her disapproval was bad but her disappointment was worse. Now I felt that same sense of unease. Why did I always push it? Is this going to be worth the risk?

One thing I had learnt though was that creativity in this industry fed the commercial beast, not the other way round. Despite Ken's alpha ego, he did give me the space to take risks. I knew looking around at the other retailers who were not making the big league that the very nature of their approach stifled creativity. You could feel their fear of making a mistake.

On the night of the pilot there's nothing Graham can do to calm me down. Takeaway curry collected, we sit on the sofa and switch on the telly.

'So what's this show about again?' he asks, pouring us each a large glass of wine.

'For the hundredth time, I've told you I don't fully know,' I answer, despairing. 'All I know is that Jennifer Saunders plays a fashion publicist and Joanna Lumley's a magazine editor. It's set in the fashion industry, and I really couldn't bear the idea that another store would gazump us and end up being featured, so I opened up Harvey Nichols for them to film the show inside. I hope I haven't blown my career by saying they could make it their stage.'

'All right, relax,' he sighs. 'What is it you always tell me? If you don't take risks, nothing changes.'

I stay quiet and press on the remote.

'This Wheel's On Fire' blares out as neon colours and block-type lettering fill the screen. Finally, it settles. '*Absolutely Fabulous.* FASHION, written by Jennifer Saunders,' I read, and we both take a deep breath. But by the time Jennifer stumbles out of bed, swigs a bottle of red wine and emerges, blinking, in her basement kitchen to find her unimpressed daughter has used her beeswax moisturiser on her toast as honey, Graham and I are belly laughing. I also know that Jennifer's 'character', Edina, is based on Lynne.

Eleven minutes in, Harvey Nichols gets its first name check. Edina and the magazine editor character, Patsy, are on their way into the office, late and seemingly woefully ill-prepared for a fashion show that's taking place that night.

'Could we go past Harvey Nicks, Eddie?' Patsy begs. 'Could we? It is nearly lunchtime.'

'It's ten-thirty, Pats,' Jennifer's character replies. 'Oh, OK. We can do Harvey Nicks quickly, pick up some lunch and take it in . . .'

Graham and I look at each other, almost seeking approval, before I hug him and breathe out a long sigh of relief. 'Harvey Nicks!' I laugh. That's what it will be called from now on, I'm sure.

I'm driving into the office the next morning, listening to the Radio 1 breakfast show. The new presenter Chris Evans is a bit chaotic, but I'll admit his energy does the job: it wakes me up. This morning there's an extra jolt.

'Sweetie, darling, I don't know what you made of *Absolutely Fabulous* last night,' he riffs, 'but I thought it was absolutely fabulous. So let's bring some fashion to this morning's show.'

I park up in Lowndes Square and retie my trainer laces, ready to start my regular run around Hyde Park. Usually, this routine helps to prepare me mentally for the day. It's normally around the halfway mark, passing Kensington Palace, that I'll tend to work out what's bothering me about the latest personnel issue or window display. Invariably it's the lighting – the hardest thing to get right. Too warm, and it begins to feel tinged with nostalgia; too cold, and the silks and tweed we're selling as luxury look cheap. Today, though, I can't settle. My pace is all off. I might think 'Harvey Nicks' is genius and will become our moniker, but that doesn't mean the board will agree.

I head back to the car early, to pick up my suit. I've gone for the YSL today. It's probably too formal for a day of internal meetings, but I needed its power. I grab the jacket hanging on the back of the passenger seat and head up to my office to change. It's only 7.30 a.m., so I'm not expecting anyone to interrupt me as I work through a pile of memos Bean has left in my in-tray. Des wants approval to ship in driftwood from Cornwall to create a beach scene for the latest Cruise collection windows. It's not naff this time – more Andy Goldsworthy-style sculptural installations – but our insurance won't cover it. They're worried about inadvertently bringing an infestation of woodworm into the store. Greta wants my team to come up with ideas as to how we can make our Estée Lauder event next month worth their investment. The beauty behemoth has just bought Bobbi Brown, the company started by the make-up artist responsible for every woman I know now wearing a nude lip, and they want to make a splash.

I'm so engrossed, I jump when Ken knocks on the door frame and sidles into my office. Briefcase still in hand, he's come to see me on his way in. That never happens.

'Well, Mary,' he says. 'I don't know British humour, but I do know that was funny. And I'm not the only one. My wife said it had everyone talking at the school gates this morning.'

Within weeks, the store is teeming with mothers and teenage daughters who've come down on the train from Kent to see what all the fuss is about. OK, they're not buying Donna Karan coats, but it's practically impossible for them to leave the beauty hall without a bottle of Clarins Eau Dynamisante for Mum or MAC's new cult colour lip gloss, Haku, for her daughter. The *Ab Fab* gamble has paid off. I try to tell myself to remember to trust my instinct, but in truth I'm already wondering how I'm going to top this.

Two queens and a roll of Sellotape

I'VE BEEN ASKED TO BE photographed as part of a portfolio of people sharing their interiors style in *ELLE Decoration* – a magazine I love. The Editor-in-Chief Ilse Crawford has revolutionised the market with her fresh take on interiors. She shoots people in their homes, not just empty, soulless rooms – wanting to show how modern Britons live today. Or at least the stylish ones. Ilse instructs her teams not to clear away every inch of clutter from the kitchens they feature and has filled her pages with ideas and inspiration from some of the hottest names in design: Tom Dixon, Nigel Coates and Philippe Starck, who has somehow managed to make even a lemon squeezer cult. I'm intrigued to see who else will be on set.

I arrive in South London to see a white Jaguar E-Type parked outside the grimy studio. Inside I find interior designer to the stars Nicky Haslam gossiping in the corner with Dame Barbara Cartland. The fag butts piled high in the ashtray imply they've already covered a lot of ground. She might have once written twenty-six novels in one year, but I've never read one of Barbara Cartland's books. Still, I know enough about the soapy romances that were a teenage Diana Spencer's favourite to recognise that Barbara looks exactly like one of her characters. Shampoo-and-set hairdo, an ostrich-plumed wrap and jewels that are so ginormous they have to be fake, she's like a doll dressed up as a ninety-one-year-old. But it's her face I can't stop staring at. She's got strips of Sellotape pulling the skin up away from her eyes right to her hairline. It gives her a strange feline look, but I've got to hand it to Dame Babs, it certainly tightens and brightens. A DIY face-lift, if you like.

'Dearest, you'll need a little dollop of something to cover up this sticky tape,' she commands the make-up artist, who is frantically searching through her kit for something matte enough to disguise the sheen.

'Me next,' squeals Haslam, grabbing the roll of Sellotape. 'Wardrobe! Where's wardrobe? Someone needs to find the end of this for me. I don't want to break a nail.'

In an industry where your face literally is linked to your pay packet, perhaps it's no surprise that everyone's on the hunt for a potion that'll reverse any signs of ageing. Or keeping a tight lid on the new colonic place to pop up on Harley Street. It was already hard enough to get an appointment for the hydrotherapy that flushed your colon with water, causing you to shit out everything that'd been stuck up there for months.

I'd tried all the so-called cult products – Clarins Beauty Flash Balm, Elizabeth Arden's Eight Hour Cream – that you could use, so the beauty editors said, on lips, cheeks and eyes. 'A true multi-tasker,' they trilled. Well, as far as I could see nothing really made a difference. Give me MAC's Russian Red and a bright red Essie nail varnish and I was sorted.

I could do without the Lancôme bronzing drops that promised a glow when added to face cream, but seemed to just turn my colleagues' finger webs a dirty shade of brown. Instead, I was drawn to brands like Aveda, which was mixing botanicals with beauty for the first time. The Austrian founder Horst Rechelbacher was a total hippie – yellow hair down to his shoulders, Dr Scholl's on his feet. He'd come into Harvey Nichols for a meeting the previous week. 'I want to create products that are good for you and good for the planet,' he'd said, before slathering my hands with a cream that smelled of tea-tree oil and holding them to his heart. 'Ommmmmm,' he chanted. I was sold.

London calling

'WHY DON'T WE MOVE TO London?' I quietly mention to Graham one Sunday in the summer as we lunch with friends in their new Islington house. Joe has bought a beautiful flat in Tufnell Park. Michael and his new wife Ros love their new house in Barnes. I want to be near them, but also nearer work, nearer the life of the city. With increasingly long days and evening events, it would make my commute easier. And at the weekends, I'd be closer to the galleries, markets and streets that give me energy and inspiration. But, also, for the first time in years my future doesn't feel distant or scary. My fear and anxiety is being replaced by a sense of anticipation, like a door suddenly swinging open to possibilities that had not been there since Mum was alive.

Graham is the man who has given me so much of that safety and love, yet I can feel his hesitancy. He's recently left his job as a chemical engineer at Unilever to become a teacher. He wanted a change of pace, and since I had started earning more at Harvey

Nichols, now secure in the idea of an annual bonus, we'd agreed that a change in his income was OK. We would manage.

We agree on a move. Not to London, but Bushey. I've found a beautiful old Edwardian house standing proudly on a corner plot framed by an ancient laburnum and a garden long gone wild. Inside, it's a wreck. It hasn't been touched since the 70s so every weekend I've been blowtorching the staircase, watching the flowery wallpaper bubble up before I can peel it off, while Graham tinkers about with the dodgy wiring. Luckily Graham isn't just beautiful and bloody clever, but is also completely comfortable working with tools, figuring out the plumbing and electrics. His combination of intellect and practical ability makes him not only a problem-solver in the classroom but a brilliant builder in our new home.

Just as at work, I love creating something from nothing: watching the elbow grease give way to a beautiful space I can furnish as I choose. That comes instinctively to me. I want colour, texture and furniture.

And thanks to the exposure to travel and events through my job, I know just where to get it. I invest in art from the RCA end of year show – abstract, colour-drenched pieces that will make our Victorian terraced two-up-two-down feel like the joyful home I've always craved. I want noise, mess, late lunches that seep into dinners. A space where people want to spend time, something my mum was always so adept at creating.

But aside from a few choice investments – art, the kind of sofa you can really sink into – I am prudent, preferring DIY to splashing the cash. Rationally I know I'm now comfortable financially, but surrounded by the levels of wealth I see at Harvey Nichols it doesn't feel that way. I'd thought the girls who were dropped off at school in Volvos, who rode ponies at the weekend, were rich. The customers I saw swan into Antonella's VIP dressing room were on another level. Personal shoppers taking them through previews of collections before they went onto the shop floor. Champagne at 10 a.m., a driver to whisk them home when they were trolleyed by lunchtime. I had discounts on every designer, flew business class and was put up in New York hotel suites with views of Central Park, but I knew it was all attached to my job. As soon as that went, so did the perks.

So while I added things to my wardrobe that helped with the day job and items to my home that helped lift me up, I did it carefully. I'd hole-punch our bank statement each month, clipping them into a ring binder I flicked through regularly, checking off receipts, watching the numbers on our account creep up. It was validation that I was doing something right at work. But, more importantly, it offered me security – and, with no family wealth to fall back on like so many of the colleagues around me, I needed that.

Ossobuco with Dolce

JUST BEFORE CHRISTMAS I'M INVITED to Milan for the launch of Dolce & Gabbana's first fragrance, Pour Femme.

Partners in business and in life, Domenico Dolce and Stefano Gabbana are becoming one of Italian fashion's most successful exports. Lace, leopard print, corsets and colour: they've bottled Sicilian sex appeal and women are lapping it up. But while catwalk collections are geared towards the wealthy 1%, or Madonna, almost anyone can buy into a designer fragrance. Most designer labels make most of their revenue from accessories – be that bags, shoes or beauty – rather than ready to wear clothes. Which is why there's practically a new designer fragrance launch a month at the moment. Opium, Obsession, Poison, Dune . . . One-word names, big business. Especially around Christmas, the prime push when a bottle of eau de toilette can be positioned as an easy gift from a lost or lazy husband.

Which is why the Italian duo are putting so much cash behind Dolce & Gabbana Pour Femme – a floral-spicy eau de toilette that comes in a crushed velvet case, red of course, that must have cost as much as the scent itself to produce.

Antonia, Becca, the fragrance buyer, and me have been flown out to Milan for tonight's dinner. We're being put up in a hotel just off the Piazza del Duomo. When I get up to my room, I find the bed strewn with oranges, little sprigs of rosemary poking out. It's a not-so-subtle way of reminding us of the top notes of the fragrance, a bottle of which is nestled in the middle of the installation. In the wardrobe hangs a gown I'll be expected to wear for dinner. They hadn't asked for my size in advance. If you don't fit into the sample, they don't want you there.

The invitation says the dinner starts at eight, but I've been to Milan enough times by now to know that no food will be served before ten. If indeed, there is food at all. More often than not, it's all foam.

'Can we grab something beforehand?' I ask Antonia, dragging her to a cocktail bar that overlooks the square's gothic cathedral. I never seem to find time to go into the Duomo on trips like this, but I love seeing the over-the-top ornateness lit up at night. We order aperitivi and fill up on pizzettes and crostini.

We arrive at the venue at nine. An hour late is just about on time in Milan. The Dolce boys have pulled some strings and we're dining in a seventeenth-century palazzo that's not normally open to the public. I spot a Caravaggio on the wall. Monica Bellucci is holding court, perched on the side of a fountain in the middle of the courtyard. She's the face of the fragrance, shot in the TV commercial lying in bed while a man stands outside her window sniffing the bra she's whipped off. When we head into dinner, she's sat in the middle of Dolce and Gabbana, who've shipped in the gilt thrones from their office for the evening.

'Mon dieu,' Antonia cries, looking at the menu resting against a pile of chillies. It's an eight-course feast, each matched expertly with an accompanying wine. By the fourth course, I am practically groaning in despair and soon end up spooning a plate of ossobuco into a napkin, to hide in my handbag.

Why do men put women down?

OVER TIME, I'D BUILT UP a wardrobe full of Dolce dresses and designer clothes that set me apart from the paint-splattered dungarees of my team. I had a trusty make-up kit: stockpiling YSL's Touche Éclat and learning to master Shu Uemura's eyelash curlers, both tools that helped turn me into the woman I knew I needed to be. I'd been given a hallowed car parking space, but I wanted a promotion. A place at the board table in my own right, not at Callum's behest. Graham and I had been talking about trying for a baby. I wanted to feel secure before I brought a child into the world. I'd been approached about a job in New York – more money, an Upper East Side rental and town car – but I didn't want to leave Harvey Nichols. If I was about to have a baby, making a move now didn't make sense. Besides, I enjoyed my job. I just wanted the same recognition from within Harvey Nicks as I was experiencing outside. Eventually, I realised it wasn't enough to play the part and hope someone noticed. If I wanted a promotion, I would have to seek it out.

I get to my appointment with Callum a few minutes early, a chance to catch up with his secretary Jessica. I know she's the lynchpin of the group of assistants who meet daily for lunch to trade titbits they've picked up.

When Callum gets there, I make my pitch. I'm now in charge of the look and feel of Harvey Nichols – from the packaging and logo on the shopping bag to events, publicity, partnerships, plus of course what we feature in the windows. It's been helping the store to squeeze more out of deals with brands, I argue, and increasing footfall and sales. Make me a director, and I'll be able to do even more. 'Plus,' I try, tactically, 'it means if my mad ideas fail, that's on me. You won't have to cover for me any more.'

'I'll support you, Mary,' Callum replies. 'But, for your own sake, you need to get on top of the numbers.'

He suggests a retail business course at the Institute of Directors that he believes will help prepare me for a world where marketing directors, sales directors and buying directors jostle for power. 'Numbers give you real power,' he cautions.

And so, a few months and dissertations later, aged thirty-two, I am asked to join the Harvey Nichols board.

I'd been in board meetings before, but always for segments, and sat on the edge of the room. Now I was at the table – albeit in the seat furthest away from Ken. I soon came to realise that board meetings were played like a game of chess; what, or who, would you sacrifice to make a successful move?

As one of only two women in that vast beige room, I also knew better than to draw undue attention to myself. Even my new seniority didn't protect me from Seb, who Ken asked to attend board meetings once a month.

At first, I'd assumed he was a bit of an Old Harrovian buffoon. The gold signet ring on his pinkie. The bold pinstripe suits worn with brightly coloured Paul Smith socks. I knew that Ken loved a posh Brit he could discuss cricket scores with. Bobbing off to Lord's with Seb and clients was a highlight.

But I soon came to realise that behind this caricature of a man lay serious ambition. Seb was a sharp and ambitious financial consultant, and it didn't take me long to realise just how ruthless he was. He had little interest in or respect for the work I did, seeing the creative side of the business as nothing more than a luxury – nice to have but certainly not essential. For him, the real priorities were the numbers, the planning and, above all, cutting budgets. That was where his power lay, and he wielded it without hesitation, making it clear that anything outside his financial remit was secondary at best. He also knew how to schmooze the people he believed really mattered. He knew Ken loved cricket and the English way of life, so he'd get tickets for a day at Lord's, making sure he was seen as both an influential consultant and a trusted friend.

I'd been asked by the *Evening Standard* to take part in a feature they called 'My London'. For the photographs, they'd commissioned Issy Blow to style me again, this time as a mannequin in the windows. The piece was a glowing endorsement of Harvey Nichols' ascent. I bumped into Seb waving a copy in his hand. 'So you think it's *your* London, do you? Goodness, that's some ego you have there, young lady.'

Another time, I turned up at work in my new prize possession, a red BMW 320, now I was allowed on the company car scheme. 'The 325 is a better model. The wife drives it. Very much a girly car,' Seb slid in as we walked into the board meeting.

As much as I tried to ignore the opinions of a man whose shirt was as yellow as his teeth, they threw me. I asked myself: why did a man need to behave like this to a young woman who was just beginning to see success?

Grunge: because sometimes the mess is the message

THAT'S NOT TO SAY SUCCESS wasn't sweet. My new role catapulted me further into the fashion world's inner circle, a place where your status was demonstrably linked to which events you were invited to. And judging by the endless 290 gsm gold-embossed cards, with their intricate calligraphy arriving on my desk, I had made it.

'Is she in the middle of an episode?' I whisper to Iain R. Webb, the Fashion Director of *The Times*, whose suit is even sharper than his tongue. We're sitting front row at the Jean Paul Gaultier show in Paris, but the uber cool stylist who works for British *ELLE* opposite me is attracting more attention than the palm prints and polka dots on the catwalk. Unlike the rest of us in Azzedine Alaïa jackets – black, sharp and serious – Anna's outfit looks like it's come from a charity shop. Baggy, sludgy men's Farah trousers, a jacket with the seams fraying, trainers and her hair chopped into a gamine, messy crop.

'That's the new look,' Iain mutters back. 'It's grunge.'

When grunge hit it was like a curtain had been drawn on the past. This was act two and out came a whole new set. The designer Marc Jacobs had been fired from Perry Ellis six months before when he'd sent plaid shirts, ditsy floral dresses and knitted beanies down the catwalk. Kate Moss, the waifish new model name to know, wore a white slip dress with heavy, unlaced combat boots. Critics had panned it. Rumour had it that Suzy Menkes, Fashion Editor for the *International Herald Tribune*, had badges made up declaring 'Grunge is ghastly'.

But, as so often happens, what the establishment hated, the generation caught up in the Courtney Love and Kurt Cobain love story lapped up and wouldn't let go. And that included my Harvey Nicks team.

I'm surprised I can't hear the hardcore thud of Nirvana and the Jesus Lizard's double a-side headbanger 'Puss/Oh, the Guilt' from my office. Cass is belting it out on full volume so that the team can hear it outside on the roof terrace. They're out there enjoying the unseasonably warm May weather while they decorate the huge panels that sit astride the escalators. These need replacing every few months and it's a ball-ache of a job. We're not allowed to stop the escalators, so the team has to lug huge canvases and mannequins onto the moving stairwells and drop them into place at just the right moment. Amputations are common.

Donald is poring over the new issue of *Vogue*. 'Look at these, Mary.'

Inside, photographer Corinne Day has shot Kate Moss against the walls of a dingy flat for a shoot titled *Under Exposure* and the pictures have landed the new editor Alexandra Shulman in hot water. The Double Ds love them – they feel fresh. In one Kate is wrapped in a quilt, wearing only a black bra. In another she poses under coloured lights that have been taped to the wall, wearing a pink tank top, lace Hennes knickers and a quizzical expression. The newspapers are whipping everyone into a frenzy. They've coined the phrase 'heroin chic', writing comment pieces implying that these pictures will spark a wave of anorexia – or worse. Advertisers are pulling their pages. Alex is having to go on *Woman's Hour* to defend her corner.

Within weeks, we've planned our next windows. We're going to turn Harvey Nichols into a dystopian warehouse. The Double Ds erect scaffolding on the street surrounding the windows, for no reason other than that we think it's a clear statement of intent. I have to reassure Callum we've asked for permission from the council – and then triple-check we actually did. Floor to ceiling, we fill the cavernous window space with concrete. I want to make it feel completely barren. We kill the lights in the windows, plunging the whole store front into darkness. A solitary model in each window is illuminated by a dull spotlight, barely distinguishable through the smoke we've pumped in.

The morning after launch, I find Antonella whispering with Antonia in the corridor. 'Lady Sutton and Sir Simon said they thought the place had been shut down,' she twitters. 'I wonder if I'm going to have to send some cards out to reassure people.'

The poshos might not have liked our take on grunge, but great art is supposed to be divisive. Besides, the new wave of designers had taken note.

Alexander McQueen's bag is from Tesco

EACH FASHION CAPITAL IS ARROGANT enough to think it is the best. New York owns optimism, but Europeans criticise the bold–as–brass brands for being 'commercial'. In other words, boring. Fashion, goes the thinking, should be about art, not sales. In Milan the eponymous designers – Giorgio Armani, Miuccia Prada, Gianni Versace, Dolce & Gabbana, the Missonis – are beginning to export their Made In Italy family businesses to the world. Meanwhile, in Paris, new designers are disrupting the established couture houses with outlandish spectacles that are as much performance art as catwalk shows. Suzy Menkes is still raving about Martin Margiela's show held in a playground on the outskirts of Paris a few years ago. Kids from the largely North African suburb sat alongside journalists on the front row as models stumbled over the dirt-strewn makeshift catwalk in boots shaped like an animal's split toe. Just as she'd schlep to the sketchier parts of Paris, Suzy will wait for designers like Azzedine Alaïa whose latest show wasn't just the standard two hours late – but two months off the traditional catwalk schedule. 'When the collection is ready, it's ready,' he'd said.

I'm biased, no doubt, but I do really believe London is where it's at for creativity. Thanks, in large part to Vivienne Westwood, the designer who's now getting global attention after taking her unique brand of Anglomania to show in Paris. Naomi Campbell tumbling over in her sky-high purple platforms made the newspapers in the UK, of course, but even *The New York Times* wrote about Westwood's, as they put it, 'divine lunacy'.

No doubt there's a touch of lunacy to Westwood. Who else collects their OBE from the Palace with no knickers on? And makes sure the paps capture the moment for posterity. But Westwood's also a cultural icon: doing as much to define Britishness as the Queen herself. Perhaps that's why the National Portrait Gallery have commissioned a piece of art where she'll be trussed up like Elizabeth I.

It's certainly why the smartest young buyers at Harvey Nichols make sure they stay close to the new British designers emerging from Central Saint Martins. And I like staying close to them. On the way to lunch, I walk past the buying office and often can't resist popping in for a chat.

Bella looks up expectantly when I pop my head around the door. She's sitting with a skinhead who's wearing baggy jeans, chains hanging off them, an oversized shirt and a scowl.

'Good timing,' Bella greets me. 'Mary, meet Lee McQueen. He

graduated from Saint Martins last year and you *have* to see what he's designing.'

I could tell she was excited. Bella took her job very seriously. Normally, she was a quiet head-down kind of girl, forensically analysing and balancing design with commerciality. I had such respect for her. For all the buyers, but particularly Bella. Their job was spotting trends: who will be tomorrow's designers, what will resonate with our middle-aged wealthy women, what's going to make us a destination and, more importantly, what's going to deliver sales. It wasn't easy.

Each week, Antonia would run through the profit margins on the individual departments. I've seen Bella, watching, waiting, picking at the dry skin on her hand until it's really red. A key installation, window or event can be enough to edge Bella's numbers into the black. And save her skin. Which is why she's so keen to bring Lee McQueen on board.

I've heard the stories about the Savile Row-trained Central Saint Martins graduate. Issy Blow bought Lee McQueen's entire graduate collection – a series of frock coats based on Jack the Ripper.

His red-hot reputation doesn't quite chime with the man in front of me slumped on his chair. Then Lee scrambles around at his feet, picking up a faded Tesco carrier bag. He pulls out a burgundy jacket that's crumpled but exquisite. I'm no Antonia, but by now I can tell a well-constructed jacket and this is just that.

Commercial, innovative and breathtakingly brilliant designers are a rare breed. There's no doubt Antonia will do all in her power to get McQueen on the shop floor at Harvey Nichols. And his tailoring will make the windows sing.

Keep the blinds up. You never know what's going on behind them

OLIVE OYL BURSTS INTO MY office unannounced. I can tell she's furious: the veins on her neck are practically pulsating through her thin, translucent skin.

'I've had enough, Mary,' she shouts. 'Cass has got to go. This is it.'

She eventually calms down enough to tell me what's happened. Olive had come in early to get a jump-start on the sales rails. The seasonal summer sale starts tomorrow, and Olive's team are already in a tizz: the clientele who come looking for cut-price Joseph aren't their favourite crowd to manage. She'd heard a kind of howling coming from the windows and approached with caution. Opening the door she'd seen Cass − butt naked aside from her Buffalos − thrusting one of the security guards like she was on stage at Madame Jojo's.

'If she thinks because the blinds are down and the windows are being refitted, that gives her permission to use the place like a whorehouse, she's not the right person for this place,' Olive concludes her four-minute rant. 'You've got to deal with it, Mary. Once and for all.'

She's obviously right. I can't have my staff shagging on office property. Or at least getting caught doing it. I'll have to read Cass the riot act.

'This is a difficult conversation, one I don't really want to have. But we're going to start here,' I tell Cass, whose booze-breath is making me gag. No one enjoys these conversations, but at least if I'm straightforward, it minimises the drama. Gets it over and done with.

I tell Cass this is her final warning: one more complaint, and I'll have no choice but to fire her. I also tell her I don't want to have to do that. She's talented.

I also tell her to remove all the window blinds. It's never sat quite right with me that we still use drapes with the Victorian-esque words 'Pardon our appearance whilst we redress this window'.

We know our customers love our window displays, so why keep the process hidden from them? It's time to let them in. Let them see the magic of their creation.

As long as Cass stays fully clothed.

New Gen

WE STOCKED THE AMERICAN BRANDS: big, brash, expert market-eers. But Ken wanted more of the Milanese brands that were becoming big hitters: exclusives on Prada's cult nylon bag collection or a first look at Karl Lagerfeld's astrological swimwear for Fendi, emblazoned with SAGITTARIUS or TAURUS. We were losing out to Harrods, who had massive buying budgets compared to us. Antonia will groan every time they throw money at designers like Jil Sander, who we're desperate to stock but Harrods have in a golden handcuff. They splash cash on securing exclusive products, which would draw customers into the store as it was the only place to see the items they'd read about in *Vogue*. And as we started drawing in talent and industry acclaim for our inventive windows and storytelling, Harrods reacted with yet more dosh: lavish dinners and takeovers of their Sloane Street façade.

I knew we'd never be able to compete with Harrods financially. So I believed we needed to lean into our creativity. Money doesn't always win out, I'd argue. Innovation can't be bought off the shelf.

My instinct was that if we could bring on board the new wave of British talent, more established ones would follow. Alexander McQueen and Hussein Chalayan were upstarts, creative and provocative, but I'd learnt that nothing motivates the fashion world more than the fear of being left behind. Even better, it would appeal to a new generation of shoppers who'd come of age under Thatcher and were drawn to the rebellious spirit of British fashion.

I knew by now that Antonia was fabulously disdainful of change, but I'd won her over with my windows by bringing her into the process and showing her we were on the same side. We both shared an appreciation for creativity – and beauty.

'I'm wary of youth. As much as I love their innovation and daring, I worry that they don't know la bonne façon,' she'd say, perched on my corner sofa, smoking, tanned legs stretched out like she was posing for a Botticelli portrait. 'But I do understand their role in the glow-up. Their essence is the essence. It's how we bottle that but balance it with the classic. That's so damn difficile.'

We're talking about how we feel the British Fashion Council isn't doing enough to support British fashion talent. Still in its infancy, the three-day-long London Fashion Week was a mish-mash of shows. The grande dame of the BFC, Annette Worsley-Taylor, seemed most at home at a Jean Muir show, where guests had their coats taken as they walked into the designer's studio and were guided to their gilt seats to enjoy the soundtrack of crooning French ballads. She'd shown up for the debut show from Bella Freud last season but then got skittish when it ran an hour late. While others in the audience whooped as Amanda de Cadenet strode down the catwalk in a pink tweed jacket carrying milliner Philip Treacy's dog Piggy, Annette checked her watch. She ran the show schedule with an iron rod. Back at her office, Annette fed the *Telegraph*'s Fashion Director Hilary Alexander Silk Cuts as she typed out her copy in her signature two-fingered style, sending her team scurrying to and from the darkroom where they'd develop photographs of the show that summed up her report.

To be fair to Annette, she had managed to get the international buyers to add London to their biannual fashion capital jaunt. But new brands were set up in a hall at Olympia, which teams from Barneys and Nordstrom would whizz around with their duplicate pads putting in orders. The brands who were able to had jumped ship to Paris: Vivienne Westwood and John Galliano showed no signs of returning to London. Every year Antonia and I would take a table at the Royal Academy of Arts end of year gala and watch the cohorts from Max Mara and Fendi eyeball talent they'd lure to Milan with big pay packets and a promise that the city understood the economic power of fashion.

'If only they'd put some money behind these young designers, it could really make a difference,' Antonia continued, on a roll now.

'Why don't we do something?' I suggest.

'I've tried. Believe me, I've tried,' Antonia replies. 'I took Annette for lunch on the fifth floor the other day. She liked the salmon fishcakes. But she's rather stuck in her ways, I'm afraid.'

'You know how you sometimes offer young designers free space on the shop floor to trial them out,' I start. 'Why don't we take that idea further and show them on a catwalk?'

'A department store staging a catwalk show? I'm not sure about that,' ponders Antonia, stubbing out her fag and lighting another straight away. 'Would anyone actually come?'

'Come on, Antonia. You know as well as I do we're not just a department store. *Ab Fab* proved that,' I shoot back. 'The industry watches the designers you're buying; people come to see our windows, our edit, our take. The best ideas are always the ones that sound mad until they don't. Let's bloody do it.

'Besides, I've ditched all those twee afternoon scones and salon-style shows. I'm talking about us getting in a proper style director to run the catwalk show. All my crew can style with the designers. We have the talent here. We could even charge some customers if we make it part of the fashion calendar. And if we did it to coincide with London Fashion Week, all the press and buyers would be in town too. Rita and Lynne could work their celeb contacts . . .'

'You know what, you're right,' agrees Antonia. 'Let's do it. Plus, we've got the space now. We could do it up on the fifth floor possibly. Nice natural light.'

When Antonia and I are both in harmony, when that mutual respect dovetails, that's when great ideas happen. We approach the fashion colleges, the RCA and Central Saint Martins, sharing the idea with Wendy Dagworthy and Louise Wilson. They're grateful for an establishment interested in supporting new talent and guide us on the best designers who have just graduated. Through them we meet a host of young designers who scuttle in with their portfolios, too shy to say more than a few words. It feels good to know that we can give them a platform.

Now we've just got to get the BFC on board.

Antonia and I approach Annette with the idea and are only half surprised when she does her usual: overcomplicates it with fake rules and regulations. We're told that if it's to be part of London Fashion Week, we'd have to slot in where they want us on the calendar. And that's Sunday, 8 a.m. And that it will also cost us thousands to be associated with them.

'That's ridiculous,' Antonia shoots back. She hates being told no even more than I do.

So we decide to go it alone. The night before London Fashion Week officially begins, we'll stage New Gen, a catwalk show at Harvey Nichols, showcasing the best of Britain's emerging fashion talent.

Antonia and I brief our teams on the idea. The successful execution will depend on their skills at negotiating and storytelling. This can't be a staid catwalk show. It needs theatre in all its forms.

Bella is tasked with approaching London's hottest new designers. Clements Ribeiro, a husband–and–wife duo who create colourful cashmere, love the idea. As does Sonja Nuttall, a Liverpudlian who's being hailed as the next Jil Sander.

When Issy Blow gets wind of what we're doing she telephones to ask if she can style a show of Philip Treacy hats. The milliner's work is incredible: his theatrical designs are already a favourite at

Ascot and he's worked with Chanel, Dior and more, but Antonia isn't sure how an entire show of millinery will work.

'Trust me, darling, it'll be wonderful,' coos Issy conspiratorially. 'And we'll get Naomi, Kate and Christy to be part of it. Everyone loves Philip.'

I'm beginning to feel we might just pull this off when Bean pokes her head around my office door. 'How are you feeling, Mary? I'm worried about you. You're taking on a lot here,' she says, giving me a stern look.

I'd told my team that I was pregnant a few weeks before. Graham and I hadn't been trying long. And while I knew that made us lucky, it had also been a shock.

I spent weeks trying to disguise how sick I was feeling, swiping the crumbs of the dry crackers I had to nibble on constantly off my desk before Bean could see, like some naughty school child.

I'd been dreading telling Callum and the team, fearing that once I did, everything at work would change – that I'd be written off or, worse, treated with kid gloves. When my body finally betrayed me and I was wearing the few outfits that fitted me on repeat, I knew I had no choice.

Callum was kind. I'd never been in any doubt that he loved his kids – a boy and girl, the quintessential family set-up – but he'd never spent loads of time talking about them. Now, he started every meeting regaling me with tales of football and ballet classes, the things he said I had to look forward to. It was almost as if now that I was going to be in the club, he could open up that side of himself.

Other than Rita, my team were bemused but sweet. Bean had assumed the maternal role, sweeping into meetings at their allocated finishing time and ushering people out of my office. 'Mary needs a little break,' she'd say, foisting another cup of ginger tea on me.

I could have done without that, but I did treasure Antonia's gift, which arrived unannounced on my desk one morning. An Issey Miyake skirt from his new collection Pleats Please and an English Eccentrics devoré top. 'You should try this,' she'd written in her signature style. 'No need to dress any differently.' The whole range was designed around concertina pleats that expanded and retracted with the wearer, meaning I'd be able to wear it in pregnancy and beyond. Immensely thoughtful and yet delivered with absolutely zero sentimentality, it was Antonia all over. I loved that skirt.

Doing the impossible is possible.
But it's bloody stressful

IT'S CARNAGE AS WE TRY to pull off the show without compromising the still-floundering fifth-floor space.

We knew we couldn't shut down the new restaurant for weeks to set up: it'd be too much of a financial sacrifice. Besides, the restaurant was now a really wonderful foodie destination. The food and beverages team had tirelessly built its reputation so that everyone who was anyone wanted to eat and be seen there.

So we'd compromised and come up with a crazy but ingenious space. The last set of escalators, leading up to the fifth floor, have been switched off and, almost overnight, we've had Jesus and a team of builders and electricians erect a white wooden catwalk filling the void of the metal staircase. The catwalk runs straight into the foyer of the fifth floor, where seats for the fashion crowd are roped off from the customers who'll still be able to get a taste of the brilliant chef Henry's cuisine in the restaurant on the other side.

Lynne Franks has been drafted in to run front of house. I watch her check the spacing for seating on the wooden bench. She sits next to a piece of paper on her right-hand side and then moves it to her left, before scooching down again and replacing her bottom with a calligraphy name placard. The only problem is not everyone who'll be front row is Lynne's size. Inevitably, the person on the end will have one bum cheek sliding off.

Backstage, trestle tables are covered in make-up and discarded coffee cups. Clothes hang from every space going, with the pictures of the model who'll wear them clipped to them. It smells of stale biscuits and burnt hair. Des has printed up T-shirts for the team to wear – a nod to us as the crew, quite literally. They're neon pink with a black-and-white photograph of their grandparents printed on the front.

'We're the new gen,' he laughs. 'Get it?'

Even Antonia is wearing one – the first time any of us have seen her in something so casual. It's sweet that she's up for dressing down despite the fact that the entire UK fashion crowd will be dolled up in their glad rags tonight. She wants to show us she's part of our crew too, and I'm touched by that and realise how much her support galvanises us all.

That said, it's me and my team who've sweated and not slept in the weeks running up to this. We've treated it like a live window installation. Every detail – from the music to the lighting and the models has been a topic of hot debate and hard work. When it became clear that we were being offered all the bland models who weren't being booked for fashion shows elsewhere, we decided to do as much as we could in-house and blow the budget on Naomi Campbell. Rigging lighting would break our backs, but a supermodel at the first-ever department store catwalk could make or break the show.

Antonia, as ever, knows nothing of this and nor does she need to. She's doing exactly what I don't like doing, wearing her sweatshirt bagging over her Jean Muir dress, air-kissing the designers and stylists who've come for a run-through before tomorrow's show.

Suddenly, Issy Blow sweeps in, her usual entourage scurrying behind her. She's wearing a McQueen minidress, five-inch stilettos and a headpiece with a giant purple feather poking out. Philip Treacy is holding her hand like he's leading her into a Viennese ball. Behind them, Issy's minions are swaying as they carry piled-up hat boxes in curious shapes and sizes along with blank mannequin head stands.

As Des gives Issy the grand tour, the team unwrap the Philip Treacy treasures. There's a gold lattice mask with a unicorn horn jutting out from the middle. A stiff piece of white leather on a fascinator is folded like a piece of origami. One is made entirely out of hand-stitched pink goose feathers. To call them hats feels like an insult. They're works of art.

'It's a disaster,' we hear Issy screech before she comes flouncing back into the room. What the fuck has Des said now? I think.

'The ceiling's too low,' she continues with her tirade. 'Once the models are in heels, the hats will hit the lights.'

'Don't panic,' I try to reassure her. 'Let's do a run-through before we panic.'

But Issy's right. The builders have fucked up. The whole set is going to have to be pulled down and reconstructed – overnight.

'Fashion is a tolerant place but I'm not going to tolerate a half-arsed show of things. You want to be here? Then acknowledge your privilege and do the fucking work,' Des lays into the builders. It's easy to see why his juniors fear and respect him in equal measure.

I should probably reprimand him for his attitude. But I know he's exhausted. I am too. The baby's just started kicking in earnest – a sign perhaps he's telling me to slow the fuck down. Rita takes one look at me and tells me to go home, get some rest.

Next morning, I'm relieved to see Issy and Philip have returned. It looks like Rita never left. The place is buzzing. Backstage, the models sip sparkling water and mainline Tic Tacs to abate any hunger as they sit through hair and make-up. Out front, every editor-in-chief and fashion director is emerging from the express elevator. I kiss Glenda Bailey hello. I love the *Marie Claire* EIC's punchy orange hair and campaigning heart. I avoid the woman from the *Express*. She's smart but drives me round the bend, always wanting inside gossip and scandal.

'Mary, can I borrow you for a moment?' Rita interrupts me as I'm about to greet Mr Valentino. I see Antonia sweep in instead, ushering the perma-tanned designer to his seat – just next to hers.

Blue lights dim the catwalk as everyone takes their seats. I never quite understand how it happens, but just before a catwalk show starts there is often an inexplicable quiet that falls. Then the music hits, the bright white light floods the catwalk and the sliding door opens. The first model stands in profile, the unicorn horn jutting out. Then she turns and strides down the catwalk as the cheers echo around. Christy Turlington, Naomi Campbell and Kate Moss follow – all in black feathered and netted numbers that float in the wind that's being blown in by a machine attached to the roof. It's a triumph.

When gambles pay off, it's easy to forget the stress, to focus on the success. And success breeds success. There's this wonderful momentum when you tap into instinct. Ideas and innovation follow. It begins to feel like anything is possible – that you're invincible. New Gen was that heady mix of hard work, clever collaboration with our colleagues in the food hall, and daring rooted in a deep sense of what felt right.

A few weeks later at the annual British Fashion Awards – the Oscars of our world – Philip Treacy scoops Accessory Designer of the Year. In his speech, he thanks Antonia for her inventive idea to launch New Gen. She beams.

Ken's in a particularly jolly mood at that month's board meeting. The Fifth Floor is finally looking like the vibrant venue he'd long hoped for, thanks to Charles and Will's hard work. I've got to hand it to them. Hospitality is tough: long, unsociable hours, tiny margins, constant pressure. But they've stuck to their guns. Continued to offer the customer experiences beyond a basic slap-up meal. And, crucially, they'd won over the hot chefs with their simple but expertly done cuisine. Once Gary Rhodes and

Marcus Wareing started dining there, the customer realised the Fifth Floor wasn't just a place to eat, but the place to be seen.

It normally benefits us all when Ken's this gung-ho. But when he congratulates Antonia for New Gen putting Harvey Nichols on the map at the British Fashion Awards, I don't trust myself to look at her. It's a reminder that, given the hierarchy we operate under, everyone is only out for themselves. Only now I've got to look out not just for me but my unborn baby too.

Nihilism, dead locusts and vodka luges

McQUEEN INVITES US TO HIS first London Fashion Week show. Antonia wants Ken to come. She's getting nowhere persuading him to entertain the idea of stocking Britain's new enfant terrible. Unlike the Calvins and Ralphs, this isn't a label with an equivalent MD Ken can wine and dine. Still, he agrees to join us at the show. The British Fashion Council are funding it – the first time they've done so for a new designer – which means Ken is astute enough to realise there will be powerbrokers in the room.

Or should I say garage: the show is set to take place in Bluebird Garage, a Grade II-listed Art Deco underground car park that hasn't been touched since the 20s. It might still have a beautiful façade, but to call the inside grimy would be kind. We've been standing around for an hour and there's no sign of the show starting.

Ken's furious. 'I'm going to be late for my table at this rate,' he scowls.

The only thing to drink is shots of vodka that come straight down the spout of a huge ice sculpture of a bottle branded by the sponsor that clearly paid for tonight's event. If the tactic was to get the waiting press hammered, it has worked. Issy Blow is tottering around, wearing a blood-red feathered McQueen mini-skirt to remind us all of her patronage. I can't work out whether her tights are intentionally ripped to shreds, but I do know that I wish I wasn't six months pregnant and the only one stone-cold sober.

'Darling, how are you?' She air-kisses me, her top hat doing its job. 'Have you seen Lee's work before? He's so marvellous. Terribly shy, but absolutely fabulous,' she continues with no hint of irony.

I feel I should introduce Ken, who's standing silently with me, still glaring. He's at his worst in an environment where he doesn't know everyone – or, more crucially, they don't know him.

'Issy, this is Ken, our Managing Director,' I try. 'Antonia's been telling him that McQueen's London's new name to know.'

'Yes, so I'm curious as to what he's all about. If he ever actually gets the show up and running,' replies Ken, shaking Issy's hand. 'Nice, er, hat. I've got one that's rather similar actually,' he adds awkwardly.

Eventually, the garage's huge doors start to wind up and we're ushered into the show space. It's pitch-black, smoke filling the cavern. Bits of paper have been stuck to the columns as a guide to where to sit. Antonia, ever the professional, guides Ken seam-lessly to our seats.

'Time to go!' she says faux-cheerfully, ignoring Ken wiping the dust off the concrete bench with his pink handkerchief.

Ominous, indistinct beats of music begin and a single spotlight illuminates the catwalk. The first Mohican-clad model emerges. She's wearing a tailored trouser suit, only with nothing underneath. Her hands clasp the jacket shut to keep her breasts covered, but it's her trousers I can't stop looking at. They're so low down her crotch there's no way she's got any hair down there. I later discover McQueen has designed them deliberately so you'll see the bum crack from the back. He's calling them 'the bumster'. The rest of the collection doesn't look any more comfortable. I can feel Ken's thigh vibrating as we watch models emerge in minidresses that look like they're made from cellophane and splattered with clay or dead locusts. Their eye shadow is red, as if they've just pulled an all-nighter. Their hair is worn in a messed-up bun, or wet and matted across their face.

'What the fuck was that?' says Ken when we finally stumble out and find his waiting Mercedes in the scrum of cars. 'It wasn't fashion, I can tell you that. You know what I'd call it?' He continues his rant. 'Obscene.'

Antonia and I look at each other as he's whisked back to Mayfair. And then we laugh. 'I'm not sure this is a fight you're going to win,' I smile.

Lady Carmichael is not a prostitute

AB FAB HAD GIVEN HARVEY Nicks global appeal – and a new customer. One I'd begun to recognise. Women who previously would have only gone to department stores (read, John Lewis) with their mother at Christmas to buy their annual bottle of Chanel No. 5 had decided Harvey Nicks was the place to be seen. They flocked up to the Fifth Floor for a post-splurge pot of tea or, more likely, a cocktail.

The circular champagne bar drew in a heady after-work crowd of loadsamoney advertising execs, girl gangs and tourists – and the odd sex worker. If they can slip in unnoticed, they know there'll be rich pickings. Or at least a round or two of drinks.

'Excuse me, madam,' whispers the white bow-tied barman to the woman perched on a high stool at the bar. She's wearing a laced corset with long fingerless lace gloves. She keeps missing the ashtray as she taps her Vogue menthol. It's hard to know if it's because she's pissed or she's not got a handle on the four-inch silver cigarette holder she's using. 'I'm afraid I'm going to have to ask you to leave.'

'Leave? Why would I have to leave?' she retorts, in a voice so plummy she could be putting it on.

'Well, madam, I don't want to make this awkward,' tries the barman, clearing his throat, 'but this really isn't the kind of establishment for women like yourself.'

'Women like me? I know the world's going anti-establishment but are you seriously telling me that Harvey's are throwing out their oldest customers?' she howls. 'Telephone down for Antonella. This is outrageous.'

Throwing Antonella's name in is enough to give the barman pause. But before he's had time to figure out what direction to go in now, the woman has tottered off – leaving her Chanel bag strewn on the stainless-steel bar.

Ten minutes later, she's back on the arm of Antonella. 'James, I believe Lady Carmichael has run into a spot of bother,' she says with her fixed, keep-calm sort-of smile. 'I've reassured her that she is of course more than welcome here any time. Now, perhaps you could fix her a gin and Dubonnet. Put it on my account.'

When you can no longer tell a Lady of the Night apart from a Lady of the Manor, you know the times they are a-changin'.

My son and me

FOR MONTHS EVERYONE AT WORK had ignored my swelling, pregnant body. Their ambivalence suited me, to be honest. I wasn't ready to get my head around the fact that I was having a baby. There was too much work to wrap up.

The personnel department hadn't figured out what it looked like when a board member went off on maternity leave – it hadn't happened before. The men who were fathers had wives and nannies at home who worried about sleep routines and vomiting bugs. But Callum assured me that the company would follow the new government legislation and pay me statutory maternity pay for three months. I'd get £52.50 a week. What he couldn't do was reassure me how work would function without me around: that was my job to figure out.

I knew I'd only be on maternity leave for three months but still I worked late every night in the run-up, sketching out window schemes for the time I'd be off, diligently filing away binders of spreadsheets, tear sheets and memos full of lengthy instructions. I figured my team would forgive my control freakiness when they came back after Christmas and realised they wouldn't be faced with a run of empty spaces.

Given my role straddled both the design team and the publicity and marketing departments, I'd never had a straight-up deputy. But I knew someone would have to step up in my absence and there was only one obvious candidate. Rita was a grown-up. She'd be able to hold her own with Ken and co., but was still respected by her staff and the design team, who loved her no-nonsense attitude. She treated them like her sons: with a lot of freedom but a healthy dose of realism when required. Most importantly, I trusted her completely. She was detail-orientated but also able to see the big picture.

I knew it would be full-on. New Gen had gone well, but we'd be doing it again in February – and sequels are often harder than debuts. 'I can't get you any more money, I'm afraid,' I explained to Rita. 'But it's good exposure. And you deserve it.'

Thankfully, she agreed. And, sweetly, set out to reassure me she'd do her best to take the pressure off me in the coming months but keep me in the loop. We agreed she'd bike window schematics to me when they were ready for approval.

'If I know you, you'll want something other than nappies to sink your teeth into. Because you don't get any feedback from babies. Other than a lot of gas,' Rita joked.

Somehow, I knew I was carrying a boy. I was so sure that I started calling him Mylo – the name that I had fallen in love with when reading Mary Wesley's novel *Not That Sort of Girl* — long before he entered the world early one icy January morning.

What I didn't know was how giving birth to my son — this edible, furrowed little man with a shock of red hair just like my mother's — would bring her back so fiercely.

As I sat Mylo in the sink for his first wash, scooping water over his bent little back, holding his fragile, stalk-like neck, I practically collapsed with love and grief. It came from deep inside me, crashing into my heart, overwhelming, unexpected and fierce. I wrapped him in his towel, sat on the bathroom floor and let myself wail like a wounded animal whose pain had been cruelly reopened by a sudden understanding of the world's most powerful love.

I ached to share this sacred experience with my mum. To see her hold my baby. To hear her voice. For her to show me, guide me. And meet her grandson. But, of course, Mum wasn't there.

No, maternity leave isn't a holiday

INCREASINGLY LOST IN A NEWBORN haze, I relied on the only two women who had kids I knew well enough to confess how much I was suffering.

My friend Kate had given birth to her third child, a son Jake, a few months before. A classic muesli mum, her kids had wooden toys, glass bottles and reusable cloth nappies because Kate was worried about polluting them with plastics. In so many ways, Kate was ahead of her time, but also well behind it.

Mylo wasn't sleeping for more than ninety minutes at a time. I wasn't sleeping at all. The relentless cycle of wake, feed, rock and then check multiple times he's still breathing was sending me mad. Since my mother had died, I'd pursued control wherever I could find it. Now Mylo was a creature I couldn't understand, let alone control.

'How long did Jake sleep last night?' I asked Kate, desperate to hear that it wasn't just me. That I wasn't a failure.

'Barely at all,' she lied back. 'It's tough, Mary. This stage is tough.

Why don't you pop him in the pram and wheel him around the block? That always worked with the girls. It's the movement – makes them think they're back in the womb.'

I bundle Mylo up and follow her advice to slide the buggy out onto the street. It's 7.30 a.m. and streams of commuters are pacing their way to the train station. I can't imagine I was ever one of them.

My sister, Tish, instinctively understands what I need. After she drops her kids at the local school she comes to mine, scooping Mylo up and sending me back to bed. I know I should be sleeping, but instead I lie awake listening to her soft whispers as she paces the hallway, chattering away to Mylo constantly. Looking after him. Loving him. By the time I surface, she's dressed him in some new hand-me-down outfit from his cousin Luke – a little racing-car-embroidered onesie or a faded hand-knitted jumper from my Aunty Cathy. As I feed him on the sofa, she kneads the dough for the soda bread Mum used to make and which we'll eat later together while watching telly. She slathers on butter so thick it could be cheese. 'Good for your milk supply,' she says, forever my bossy big sister.

When she leaves to start her nursing shift, the loneliness hits again. Graham had a week off work – and one of those days was the day I gave birth. Now I spend long, dark, silent afternoons waiting for him to come home. Praying he won't be later than he said he would.

It's almost a relief when the doorbell goes and a courier hands over a supersize envelope. Rita has sent me another bundle of paperwork to review. As Mylo snoozes next to me in bed, I sign off ideas for sunny, summer window schemes or scribble suggestions for next season's product launches.

In some ways, the fact that I never really stop working makes the idea of going back to Harvey Nichols easier. Workwise, I know exactly what to expect. Except I don't. The window schemes might be sorted, but how will I be as a boss now I'm also a mum? I don't know how I'll work at the same pace as before, how I'll switch into that gear. I don't even know what I can wear with cabbage leaves stuck in my bra.

'Look, the truth is everything has changed. You can never go back to how it was before because you're not the same. But that doesn't mean you can't make it work,' Rita reassures me when I confess how I'm feeling. 'Trust me, the thought of coming back is worse than the reality.'

She's here to talk me through an event for the McQueen launch. Antonia and Bella won: we'll stock a select range of McQueen's jackets this season. I'm supposed to be helping unpick the politics of a seating plan, where so-and-so can't possibly be placed near her latest sworn enemy.

'Doesn't she just need to get over herself?' I eye-roll as Mylo starts screaming for a feed. 'I really haven't got the tolerance for this any more.'

'And that's exactly why we need you back in the building,' Rita shoots back.

I've been interviewing for a nanny for weeks now, but I can't reconcile the idea of leaving my three-month-old son with a stranger. The agency I've signed up with sent over a list of suggested questions I should ask at an interview, but I don't want to know what her approach to discipline, sleep training or weaning will be. All I want to know is whether she'll love Mylo, that he'll be safe.

Eventually, I choose Susannah, a Northern Irish woman in her twenties. She's so quiet I can barely hear her when she runs through her qualifications, but she makes me feel calm and that's what I want around Mylo.

'Careful when you go down the stairs into the kitchen, especially when you're holding him. They're slippery,' I tell Susannah, talking her through the peculiarities of the house in our week's handover before I go back to work. It's so odd training someone to take my place. Going out to browse aimlessly in the local bookshop just to give her an hour in the house with Mylo by herself.

The night before I'm going back to work, I let Mylo fall asleep on my chest. I sob, but silently — I don't want the vibrations to wake him up.

'I'm leaving him with someone I've known for a week,' I cry to Graham, shell-shocked. There's not much he can say. We both know I have to go back.

'Have a good break?' Seb asks at my first board meeting with a smirk.

I can't work out whether he's joking, or ignorant enough to actually think that three months where it feels like your body is splitting or leaking is a break. I smile and unsheath my Mont Blanc pen. 'It's nice to be back. I'm glad you coped without me,' I reply.

Ken comes to me first. I've asked him to add a point to the agenda. I want to put Rita forward for a bonus. 'She's worked exceptionally hard. The results are testament to that,' I start before running through her accolades. I'm grateful that she's kept my department afloat and think she deserves some financial reward, given she didn't get anything extra in my absence.

'I take your point, Mary,' Ken cuts in. 'But, where I stand on it, is that if you start with one, it sets a dangerous precedent. One we can't afford.' He puts it to a vote, but with a precursor like that no one is going to side with me.

It's clear that nothing at Harvey Nicks has changed. But I have. I feel completely different. So how's that going to work? I wonder.

I didn't waste my time on things I didn't love

EVERY MORNING BEFORE I LEAVE the house for work, I say a silent salute to a photograph of a pregnant me hanging on my bedroom wall. I'd asked Terry O'Neill to take some pictures of me just before Mylo arrived. I wanted to remember the moment. Commemorate it. My hair is cropped – I'd had Joe chop it all off so I wouldn't have to mess around with it when I had my hands full with the baby. I'm looking straight into the camera. I'm smiling, but there's both an uncertainty and a determination in my expression. Even then, before I'd felt Mylo's soft, warm breath and heartbeat up against my chest, I'd realised that becoming a mother would make me more driven to succeed. To build a life for him, for our family.

It's why I throw myself back into work, eager to understand what's hot, what's not and what I can impact – quickly. I've realised I cannot work in the same way as I once did. As much as I loved working late into the night, enjoying the stillness of a department store once the doors are shut, now I want to be home for bedtime and bathtime as often as I can be. And that means there's no time to waste in my day. Long lunches are over; I'll eat at my desk. I learn the art of ruthless prioritisation: throwing all my energy into high-impact tasks, eliminating pointless ones and saying no to distractions. I time-block parts of my day so I can work with absolute focus. I start to delegate in a way I'd never done before, deputising and sending Rita into meetings where I know I'm not essential. I have utter faith in her ability to take responsibility. I haven't been able to give her a bonus, but I can ensure she maintains the visibility and opportunities to prove herself that she'll need to get promoted.

I put in a request to add to my team. I'm going to need all the help I can get and I already know who I want: Callum's personal assistant, Jessica. There are two other women under Rita in the marketing and publicity team. Nicole is the social butterfly: the whiff of a free champagne and she'll be out. Every morning, she comes in with a new story, a connection she's made. By contrast, Sylv isn't a born networker, but she's a grafter. If you want shit done, you ask Sylv. Now I need someone who has ideas, a fresh perspective, but also the energy to support Rita.

I have a pile of CVs from people desperate to join Harvey Nichols; they know a position here gives them a platform for their creativity. Antonella is also constantly bombarding me with requests from Lord and Lady Want-A-Lot who have a great-niece once removed they think really does deserve a break. But I've seen Jessica's hunger and I admire it. She has great organisational skills and a beautiful manner with people. More importantly for me, she'd used her holiday days to come and sit with us, eager to learn, muck in and suck up every bit of insight from my talented team. 'Do you think I could ever join you?' she'd asked me last year, bringing me endless cups of tea.

Still, when I offer her the job, she has that doubtful female response I've seen so often. 'Me? Are you sure? I don't have any experience.'

'You might not have officially worked in publicity and events before, but you've proven to me you really want this,' I reply. 'You're committed and curious. That's what I'm looking for.'

I'd checked with Callum before offering the job to Jessica, of course. He'd been magnanimous. 'I mean finding a good PA's harder than finding a decent wife, but she's done her time and she deserves growth,' he'd sanctioned.

Jessica's proven us both right – and done herself proud. She's furiously efficient but also good fun. Rita is happier than I've seen her in years. And that makes my life easier too.

I'm learning that leveraging these support systems, asking for help, doesn't feel like a weakness – it simply helps me be efficient and stay focused. When I'm at work, I'm concentrating on the absolute top priority. When I'm at home, I'm watching Mylo learn to crawl, opening every drawer he can reach with wild abandon. When he's in bed, I'm at the kitchen table catching up, trying to anticipate what the next big thing I should focus my energies on is.

Beauty is booming. We have reconfigured the ground floor to accommodate the sexy new brands that are literally on everyone's lips. Stila is one, the make-up brand that's captured the youth market with its sugary-sweet range of lip glazes and cutesy packaging featuring hand-drawn pen-and-ink pictures of a globe-trotting gal. 'Pretty in Paris' reads one. 'Make an impression in Moscow', another. London girls have gone wild for the vanilla lip gloss that you click from the tube up into the brush. The team and I have adopted a flexible layout to the shop floor so we can quickly adjust and accommodate all these emerging trends.

At the other end of the spectrum, Dior has created an entirely new market with its Svelte range designed to tackle cellulite. The Svelte Body Refining Gel sold out worldwide last year, with 100,000 bottles apparently being snapped up in the first two days it went on sale in Japan. Greta has volunteered to be the guinea pig for their new Svelte Perfect, a more complex cream that promises even better results – for double the price.

'It is really important that here in the beauty department we fully understand what we're selling,' she says before scarpering with the sample. 'We're a trusted institution, after all. We need to know we can endorse what's on our counters.' I didn't remind her about her attitude towards Aveda.

But, all the interlopers aside, Becca tells me that MAC still reigns supreme, with customers continuing to pour in for their punchy pigments and palettes. She also says Frank and Frank have come up with another of their harebrained ideas: to launch a new lipstick with all the revenue going to a charity fighting AIDS.

'It's a brownish blue-red shade. They're calling it Viva Glam,' she tells me when I run into her having a fag out the back of the loading bay. Bar the odd social cig, I've never really smoked, but I come out here from time to time to catch my breath – and hide. Before Mylo was born, whenever someone was bearing down on my office who I didn't want to see, I'd climb out of the window onto a teeny terrace that ran along the entire back of the window. Back to the wall, I'd edge along until I reached the buying department's office at the end of our corridor and climb into their retreat. They were all eccentric and on-edge enough not to notice how mad it looked to see my suede Manolo mules appear over the window sash. But since giving birth, I've become afraid of heights. So, much to Bean's annoyance, I now get my peace amongst the skips and security guards out back. Bean won't venture down to the basement to fetch me, claiming it's too cold. I'll come back to see my desk covered in Post-It notes from her – increasingly erratic in their detailed messages of the visitors or calls I've missed.

'The *really* revolutionary thing is that MAC is giving 100% of the revenues to charity, not just the profits,' Becca continues.

She's right that launching a new product you'll make no profit from is bold. But that's not the only thing that makes it revolutionary. Despite the fact that we've all seen the trauma of the HIV epidemic ripping through the world, AIDS isn't a hot subject. Far from it. There's still so much homophobia, whipped up by establishments who blame gay men for what they call the modern plague.

We all know someone who has died of AIDS. Over the last decade, we've become used to the whispers that spread through offices. 'Ian died yesterday. He was only twenty-eight,' someone

219

will sombrely state. There will be a day when a handful of the display team are missing – at the funeral of a man they went to college with. We'll cover for them, knowing instinctively that it's easier if the bosses don't know the truth of where they are.

The trauma of the 80s has affected us all, but for some of my team it's more personal – more pressing. It's obvious that Donald is gay. But, unlike Des, who'll boast to anyone who'll listen about his wild nights clubbing in Heaven, Donald doesn't discuss anything personal with me, certainly not his love life. Sometimes I wish he would. It would make it easier when I have to hide his unexplained absences from Callum, when his migraines hit, or excuse his spurts of sullen moodiness that prompt Olive Oyl and her team to go on the warpath. But I understand Donald's desire for discretion. Section 28 has made everyone paranoid, increased the shame and the secrecy. At one Christmas party, a vodka-fuelled Des had launched into a story about Donald's vow of celibacy. 'His partner's ex died and it haunted them both. They couldn't find a way to stay together, so . . .' he started before breaking off and changing the subject. Des was a livewire but he was also a good friend. He knew he'd over-stepped, and we both knew never to mention it again.

I approach Des about Viva Glam. 'The Franks are using their platform to help raise awareness of and funds for the AIDS epidemic, and Becca is right to be trying to get Harvey Nichols involved. We can help them launch it in the UK,' I tell him.

'Oh, I know, it's fabulous,' says Des, who already knows the score. 'They've got RuPaul in the campaign. Have you seen it? He's hot,' he adds, fanning himself.

I seek out the office copy of American *Vogue* to find the campaign. It's the first time a beauty brand has used a drag artist. RuPaul poses in a beehive platinum-blonde wig, a red leather corset and thigh-high red patent boots. They look sweaty.

True to MAC's DNA, the campaign is provocative, but with purpose. MAC's co-founders, Frank Toskan and Frank Angelo, have been saying in interviews they want the lipstick to be a loud and proud declaration of protest, but also to raise money for homeless shelters and soup kitchens that help victims of the AIDS epidemic. It's typical of them to have tapped into the new movement of gay men who are visibly, publicly trying to counter the stigmas that have haunted the community for so long. Gianni Versace and Elton John are showing the world that you can be proudly gay, talented, successful global superstars.

A trip to Canada and a boatload of vodka later, we have a plan with the MAC boys to launch Viva Glam in the UK. We'll fly over RuPaul and MAC's top make-up artists will do his make-up live in window 12 – the prime slot – before a catwalk show where designers will create outfits inspired by the lipstick's shade.

I'm uncharacteristically nervous before the big day, fussing over the lighting and ripping up the mark made from parcel tape on the floor that indicates where RuPaul will sit. 'Oh, stop fussing, will you?' says Donald calmly. 'The crowds, they'll come.'

I suspect it has more to do with Rita placing a call to the *Evening Standard* news desk that morning than Donald's manifestation, but the crowds do indeed come. They're twenty deep on the street outside, watching as RuPaul is transformed with facial tape, brow glue and false lashes so long they need to be trimmed like a Schnauzer.

'Can you ask Harold to radio up for some extra security?' I ask Rita. I'm worried about the scrum blocking the pavements. The last thing we need is someone getting hurt – or the council getting called.

When the make-up artist slicks on RuPaul's finishing touch, a glossy layer of Viva Glam, the doors open. The crowds surge in, eager to be first to spend £15 on a piece of beauty history, and jostle into the catwalk space.

From backstage I can see the mix of MAC devotees and curious fashion press opening the matte black boxes and trying their Viva Glam. There is a ceremonial, communal feel as people hand around compact mirrors so people can check their smears.

RuPaul is getting ready to host the show when Bean scurries in. My nanny has called to say that Mylo has a fever that's not coming down with Calpol and he's just been sick. I'm supposed to be on stage in five minutes to introduce the show.

'You have to go, Mary,' says Callum kindly. 'Don't worry. You've got it to this point; this is all you. But now Mylo wants his mum, and we can handle it. Go.'

As I rush upstairs I hear Callum take my place. 'Mary Portas was supposed to be here instead of me,' he tells the crowd, with a little laugh that tells me he's far out of his comfort zone presenting to a bunch of transvestites and fashion directors.

I'm grateful – both for the acknowledgement and him stepping in. It means that I make it home in time to lay cold compresses on Mylo's forehead and murmur calmly to him. Even if, as I lie on the bathroom floor still in my Jil Sander suit, I know it's only a matter of days until Mylo's norovirus will hit me too. Can I really make a job like mine work now I have Mylo? At least with my sanity in check.

Bunking off

THE CHAIRMAN LIKES TO TAKE August off; it's the only time he can get a proper run around Europe on his yacht. That means we have to work the weekend – again – to present him with the Q3 plans so he can get up to speed before he speedboats off.

Mostly, the Chairman stays put in the C-suite. Steaming pots of coffee and cocoa-dusted truffles come to him, wheeled up by the facilities staff on trolleys, as do a steady stream of people with their manila folders of ideas and budgets. But, occasionally, he likes to 'walk the floor' – come downstairs to our corridor to surprise us, get a sense of what we're like in situ. The first time I see this play out, I realise it's why Antonia has organised her offices with the precision of a shop-floor manager putting out new season Gucci. Her PA, Tina, is stationed just by the lift, after which comes her office and then that of the buying team. Tina is under strict instructions to greet the Chairman courteously but loudly, stalling him by offering a cup of tea we all know he won't accept. That gives Antonia time to emerge from her office – pausing only for a spritz of L'Eau de Néroli – and walk up to greet him, effectively ambushing him before he gets to her buying team. Antonia might not be afraid of balling them out in their monthly revenue meetings, but she knows enough to protect them from unfettered contact with the bosses. I admire her foresight and tactics. After all, no one is doing the same for her.

It doesn't occur to Ken and co. that Antonia has sacrificed her personal life to ensure she's at the top of her game. The job is her plus one. She spends weeks living out of a suitcase for the catwalk shows. She's the one who will drop everything to be on Concorde when someone's needed to scope out a new potential business opportunity. It's the reason she's one of the most respected women in fashion.

The more I understand Antonia, the more I respect her and come to count on our alliance. Like all the best work partnerships, there would always remain a sheen of competition between us. We both knew that was helpful: that clashes, a bit of healthy combat, would continue to push us and our ideas forward. But we equally appreciated that, alongside that rivalry, we could build a friendship. Besides, we were the only women on the board, and I think both of us had begun to realise that we were stronger together rather than divided.

'Fancy sloping off to the movies?' Antonia says mischievously, appearing at my office. It's 11 a.m. on a Monday. 'We *have* been working all weekend,' she justifies, closing the door quietly. 'And, quite frankly, I've had it up to my eyeballs with this place.'

I can't help laughing. 'Antonia, we've worked together for years, and I had no idea that you do this!' I reply, pleasantly surprised to see this side of her.

'Does that mean you're in?' she deadpans back.

We grab our coats and stride out purposefully, both telling our PAs the other is taking us to their meetings. We know they'll talk and figure it out, but it doesn't matter. We have a date at noon with *Forrest Gump*.

'Stupid is as stupid does,' we repeat to each other as we stumble out of the arthouse movie theatre onto Sloane Street afterwards, sobbing. It's still light, but there's no way we're going back to the office after that gut-wrenching watch.

'Drink?' I suggest.

'Absolutely,' Antonia replies.

We grab a cab and head to the Atlantic Bar and Grill. Oliver Peyton's Art Deco restaurant only opened a few months ago but it's already the hot ticket. Given it's 3 p.m., we reckon we'll get a table.

When Antonia orders Long Island Iced Tea – double the calories of her usual vodka – and throws down £20 notes, it's clear she's in a reckless mood.

'I tip generously,' she explains. 'I tip attractive waiters and waitresses very generously because it's good to be on the side of victory.'

We drink and drink, laughing and bitching about Ken's shoes and taste levels. When Jeannie from Issey Miyake and her boyfriend come in for dinner we're still there and end up joining them for prawn cocktails and chocolate mousse.

The celebrities love that the Atlantic Bar and Grill has a late licence, but we're less keen when we stumble out at 1 a.m. to the waiting paparazzi. They hoped to snap Madonna — instead, we're two women who definitely can't go home in this state. I call Graham to beg forgiveness. I just needed to let off some steam, I explain. As ever, Antonia takes charge, leading me to Duke's hotel — and handing me a key to a room for the night.

The next morning, we arrive early at the office to sheepishly raid the fashion cupboard for clean underwear and a change of clothes. I choose to borrow a fabulous Byblos multi-patterned silk wrap top with orange shorts for the day, and don't regret a thing.

What if we give rather than take?

IT'S OCTOBER, AND I'M PRESENTING my latest idea for Christmas windows to the board. Their silence suggests it isn't going down well. Admittedly, it is radical: giving over fifty metres of prime retail space to nothing but a white plinth with a sign saying which charity has benefited from the money that would have been spent on installing the Christmas windows.

'Why the fuck would we do that?' is Ken's immediate response. No surprise there. 'We're in the retail business. We sell stuff. That would put people right off. People want to be indulged at Christmas when they come here, not turn up to a store with jack shit in the windows.'

My argument is that in a world which is heaving with ostentatious displays of wealth, customers would respond positively to a message of charitable giving at Christmas.

'It'll get cut-through,' I argue. 'We want impact. Every store has upped their window display budgets and they're using the power of windows to a really extravagant level. I want us to go against the norm.'

I really do believe in this idea. But this is also my sixth year planning Christmas displays, and if I'm honest, it's my least favourite brief. I've set a level of expectation with the public and the press. I need to capture the glamour and glitz of Christmas but also keep the essence of Harvey Nichols: witty or whimsical. Shoppers flood into the West End at this time of year – the latest stats show footfall was up 40% last December – so the competition is fierce to capture the biggest slice of this swelling, lucrative audience.

Last year, I'd collaborated with Tim Burton, the director whose mind is a maelstrom of genius. It was rare for me to do this; collaborations have to have a true, symbiotic relationship otherwise they can feel really naff. But I loved *Beetlejuice*, Burton's gothic comedy film. It was so weirdly original that it worked. So when his team approached me about styling windows to coincide with his film *The Nightmare Before Christmas*, I agreed. When Burton came in to see the space and tell me about the concept of Jack Skellington, who decides to sabotage Christmas, he was everything I'd hoped for, and the final window displays were equally crazy, weird and very Harvey Nichols.

Some of our windows of Christmas past had been graphic, bold and minimalist. Jesus the carpenter had built huge triangular moulds and, one summer, the team poured in resin and hundreds of Quality Street to set them into shapes they could then construct in situ as Perspex Christmas trees. I'd noticed there were no purple sweets in the final set – they had obviously been the favourites amongst Cass and co.

Others had been ornate and playful, designed to capture the imagination of both harassed mums holding their toddlers' sticky hands and the Knightsbridge elite. For our sexy Circus theme, we had spinning mannequins in leopard print and top hats hanging from the ceiling. Red roses and black netting covered the floor, inspired by a Dolce & Gabbana Basque show I'd attended that year.

'Peas on earth' had really made me laugh: we'd created huge papier-mâché models of peas and styled all the mannequins in varying shades of green and white. It was stark but incredibly visual.

Now I want to do something with feeling. Something purposeful.

'I know it's radical. But it will show our customers we stand for something,' I try again. 'Callum, what do you think?' I am trying to be patient, to build consensus in the room, but instinctively I know this is right, and I resent having to wade through so much bureaucracy.

His attention span waning, Ken signs off the idea, as I knew he would. I've proven that even my most madcap schemes have paid off so have earned his trust, but it still feels like he has to pontificate and showcase his knowledge while I nod and agree.

It's hard to believe the amount of people involved in creating one window, especially one that is so deliberately simple. Jules works out the best shade of white paint, factoring in the impact of bright lights and accumulative dust. She practises her calligraphy

WHAT IF WE GIVE RATHER THAN TAKE?

for weeks before we even work out what we're going to say. We want it to feel like a Christmas card from the Queen. It has to be powerful but not make people feel guilty for spending. It needs to touch their hearts and share their joy, rather than put them off. So we decide on something honest and simple.

At least we don't have to send the mannequins back to Rootstein to have their summer tans stripped back to the pasty skin we've all got by this time of the year. That saves a lot of budget, and the money goes in the charity coffers. There's no need to bother Olive Oyl and her team of floor managers to pull clothes for the window displays. This year there'll be no fights about which of her precious gowns she can relinquish from the shop floor for the window display.

What we do need is help. We wanted to commit all the budget we would usually spend on the Christmas windows to charity. That meant persuading Farrow & Ball to donate paint, the team sacrificing any overtime pay and the fabric company we relied on for backdrops providing the felt for free.

We also need a consensus on the charity we're going to support. I can see Rita wheeling back and forth to Jessica's desk, debating the merits of each.

'What about Oxfam?' Rita suggests. 'Everyone knows their work, so we won't have to explain why we're supporting them.'

Then it dawns on me. 'Why only one charity? Let's use each window to support a different charity,' I say. 'Save the Children, Oxfam, the children's hospital Princess Diana took Christmas presents to . . . There's no way Ken will fight that one.'

It's exciting to think we could split the budget in a way that would make meaningful contributions to a higher number of charities. Decision made, Des, Donald and Jesus wheel the plinths down the lifts and into the windows, drilling and screwing them securely into place before touching up the damage and hoovering the sawdust. 'This year we've chosen to donate the money that would have been spent on these windows to Great Ormond Street Children's Hospital. Happy Christmas, kids' reads one.

I'm nervous about the reaction to the radical Christmas windows. I worry that I've taken the indulgence out of Christmas and that it will leave people feeling guilty. Then I think, good, guilt is the cost of conscience. Maybe our actions might even prompt customers to donate money to these charities too. Rita lines up endless interviews for me to justify the decision. She comes prepared, trotting out the figures hitting the charity coffers from a memo she'd pulled together for us as briefing notes. It feels faintly ridiculous discussing our charitable endeavours over the starched white tablecloths of Claridge's.

But the business press love the Christmas charity windows. *Campaign* magazine nominates it for best campaign of the year. More importantly for Ken, it doesn't seem to have put shoppers off. Olive Oyl reports that customers are telling the girls on the counter they're moved by the message, and once they're in the store they're spending – perhaps appreciative of what they have and who they love.

For me though, the most significant response to our windows comes from the charities themselves, who write to tell us how the money will be spent. Then, one of the Great Ormond Street directors – a doctor who specialises in blood and bone marrow transplants – phones to ask if he can bring some of his patients to see the windows. I'm not sure there's much for kids to look at, I tell him, but when a group of them arrive, kitted out in festive blankets, their faces tell me otherwise.

'It's recognition they matter,' one of the parents tells me as we huddle around the window as it starts to sleet. The candy canes and hot chocolates topped with whipped cream Jessica has cleverly thought to bring down from the café don't hurt either. We give the parents a Christmas pudding to take away and throw in a few extras for the nurses and doctors on the wards. They won't get much of a Christmas break.

I love my job when it's like this. The mix of people, experiences – the access creativity and curiosity open up. One day, a fashion designer. The next, doctors saving lives.

I shut down my computer at lunchtime on Christmas Eve and drive home for the festive break feeling proud.

But, at home, a burst water pipe has flooded the kitchen and Mylo is howling. Ever the practical one in our partnership, Graham hands me the baby and gets his tool kit out, knowing we'll never get a plumber to come at Christmas.

My siblings are all arriving the following morning and there's still food to get in, so I strap Mylo into his buggy and we walk to Sainsbury's. I find supermarket shopping strangely soothing, even on a frenzied Christmas Eve. It's a comforting ritual for me, doing such a simple, practical grounding act as filling a trolley of food for my family. My friends think I'm mad, but there is a reassurance in knowing my cupboards will be fully stocked, my home will be my safe space and soon I'll be sitting around the kitchen table laughing with my siblings while Mylo crawls around the floor with his cousins. If only Mum could see us all. She'd love it. And tell us we've steamed the Christmas pudding too long.

Tom Ford doesn't wear pants

THE FUNNY THING ABOUT FASHION is that, for an industry built on newness, its calendar has remained the same for ever. All of which means it's February and the same group of editors, buyers and stylists are on their way to Milan for Fashion Week – seven days of shows, dinners and cocktail parties on a schedule that's a carbon copy of the previous year. It's hard not to feel jaded.

I'm unpacking in the Principe, the new hotel to stay in during Milan Fashion Week. Invitations and white roses are piled on the table. I haven't got Antonia's influence, but I've reached a point where cloying publicists think it's worth flattering me. As I arrange the pile of clothes I need to be steamed, I find Pengi – the ratty penguin that belongs to my now one-year-old son. It's his favourite toy, the one he sleeps with religiously. My heart lurches. Last night, he'd refused to go to bed. I told myself he was too small to realise that I was leaving, but perhaps my anxiety about leaving him spread by osmosis. I sat on his floor and held his hand until his steady, slow breathing told me he'd drifted off. I've no idea how the toy has found its way into my suitcase, but by now it's 7 p.m. in London. I'm stricken with guilt that he'll have another sleepless night, but there's nothing I can do. I have a Gucci show to go to.

Restless fashion critics are keen to see what Tom Ford will do at Gucci after his first dud season. There are still high hopes that the Texan can restore the heritage brand to its glory days. He needs to; the news on the ground is that Gucci have been struggling to pay their staff as business is so bad.

Afterwards, Antonia has organised a dinner with Tom Ford and his team at Bice, a low-fi restaurant with paper tablecloths that fashion people love because it allows them to be the most pretentious thing in the room.

I'm under strict instructions from Antonia to help get them over the line on supplying exclusives for the new season. But since Des let me in on the rumour that Tom Ford doesn't wear pants, I can't imagine how I'm going to talk shop and keep a straight face.

'You've got one job,' were Des's final words to me as I left the office. 'I need to know what side he dresses on.'

As the show begins I can't help but think Des will approve of this achingly sexy collection. Jewel-tone satin shirts are worn unbuttoned to the naval. Velvet low-slung, skinny trousers in navy, orange and chartreuse look expensive – and exposing. I watch as *Vogue's* chief critic Sarah Mower scribbles in her notebook: 'one of those hitting-in-the-solar-plexus moments.'

The place erupts as Tom Ford appears to make an unsanctioned bow at the finale. We've heard rumours it's in his contract that he's not to appear at shows: one man must not overpower the mega brand.

Within months, the high street is filled with purple synthetic shirts that teenagers wear out clubbing with black tailored trousers, blissfully ignorant that they've succumbed to the Tom Ford effect – albeit the flammable version. Madonna wears the real thing at the MTV Awards, thus anointing the suave American as the new king of fashion. Customers are flocking into the store, squeezing into the only tiny sizes we have left.

Antonia is thrilled. All I can think about is the dinner we'd had after the show. Tom had arrived late and knocked back two glasses of prosecco in quick succession.

'I'm glad you liked it,' he'd told Antonia graciously. 'It was a risk. But, let's be honest, when things are that much of a mess you can do anything. I just took advantage of the freedom.'

My focus wasn't on his gamble though. It was firmly on his velvet trousers. Note to self: tell Des it hangs stage left.

Linda Evangelista is in the window

MOST OF OUR WINDOW DISPLAYS were to drive footfall into store. Some were to launch exclusives. Others to position Harvey Nichols in a new light, to create a piece of art or prop up Estée Lauder. But the window we were working on now was, in all honesty, because I wanted an excuse to work with Linda Evangelista.

I'd run into Linda at one of Donna Karan's cocktail parties in New York the year before. She'd opened the DKNY show and was one of the guests invited to Donna's Upper East Side penthouse to celebrate afterwards. Despite the fact that it was February and freezing, we'd both found ourselves outside on the terrace that overlooked Central Park. As we peered down at the procession of town cars crawling down Madison Avenue, their fur-festooned passengers emerging like ants as their vehicle reached the awning, we found ourselves getting dizzy.

Up close, Linda was gorgeous – so glossy. Perfect teeth, skin, hair, but also that athleticism that I loved about the original supermodels. My team were crazy for the Brit girls that'd broken through – waifish Kate Moss or kooky Karen Elson. I had to admit I loved Stella Tennant, the granddaughter of Deborah Mitford. But I still had the biggest crush on Linda. She was in another league.

I often had crushes on women. I had never fallen in love with one, but, surprisingly, as I got older and more confident, the idea of being with one crossed my mind. When I'm around women I feel so much more relaxed. I am able to be fully me, not diminish myself to make the societal expectations of male ego feel OK, nor stretch myself to fit into the alpha world of business. I feel free.

Weeks later *Vogue* get in touch to ask if they can use the windows to shoot the best of the spring/summer collections. Nick Knight is the photographer, Linda Evangelista the model. For me, it's a no-brainer.

Nick is notorious for his beautiful, expressive photography, his constant pursuit of newness – and his exacting standards. He once laboured for two months over a Jil Sander campaign, something I can only imagine didn't go down brilliantly with the marketing director. As we discuss his ideas on a recce of the store, I recognise Nick's restlessness, his energy. He has strong ideas about what he wants: a lime-green shell, open at the back so he can shoot Linda looking onto the street. He wants onlookers in shot but not staged: real people passing and captivated by the supermodel throwing shapes in the window. I don't think he'll have to fake that, but I know that security will have to be tight if we're to pull this off. And we'll need to do it at the end of the day, when the store is closed. Linda is a major star, a regular on the covers of British *Vogue* thanks to her selling power on the newsstand. The last one she did, shot by Nick, with its flashy ring light and 'Very Versace: the story of a £6,000 dress' headline, was heralded by *The New York Times* as signalling the end of grunge and the return of glamour.

Linda herself arrives with little fanfare. Antonella has vacated her VIP dressing room to act as *Vogue*'s makeshift studio. Linda is zoned out listening to her Walkman as multiple make-up artists paint her nails and start her make-up. They're giving her the full Marilyn blonde-bombshell look. Fashion assistants steam the endless rails of pastel clothes, but I'm always surprised by how few will actually be worn and shot.

Des's hovering, of course. He won't miss a chance to get some stories about Linda to regale the pub with later. So he practically melts when Linda, taking charge, strips off the white Giorgio Armani top she's wearing and asks for his help. 'Could you be an angel and get the creases out of this?' she says, wearing just her bra and a pair of low-slung jeans. Des doesn't know where to look. But he does know where to find an iron. Within minutes, he's back with the top so starched his mother would be proud. Linda flashes him her famous smile, slips it on and struts to the window.

Nick has positioned his lighting assistant on the street so the flash shines through the window making the lime-green floor look fluorescent. He doesn't need to give Linda instruction. She lies down, eyes closed, head lolling like she's in ecstasy and pulls her top up past her rib cage. She arches her back slightly, and Nick starts shooting. At first, passersby keep doing just that – walking straight past. But with each flash of the camera, they're drawn in like moths to a flame, until suddenly the street is packed. Kids in bombers and baggy denim jackets and women wearing drab coats are soon crammed against the glass. They're all looking down on Linda like she's an angel. Which of course, to us, she is.

As Linda cycles through outfit changes, the crowds build. By the time she's in the showstopper – a crushed pink satin Prada gown – stretching out her hands on the glass, it's hysteria.

It's not often you recognise you're in a culturally defining moment when you're actually living it, but watching the frenzy unfold I knew instinctively that this was one. Outside, the crowds are screaming. Inside, Nick is working meticulously, silently, creating pictures that tell a story, that capture a mood. Fashion has become entertainment. Shopping isn't just about filling your wardrobe with stuff or scrolling through endless pages of products online, but about feeling you're part of something. The Harvey Nichols we've created is a space for people to connect. Coming here is as much about being part of a creative, buzzing scene as it is leaving with a new shirt and a monochrome carrier bag. People on the street are being let into the secrets, the sex appeal and the glamour – and, more often than not, they're the ones shaping it. We are in an era of original ideas and even more outrageous behaviour.

Put your hands around his balls . . . and squeeze

I SPEND SO MUCH OF my working life surrounded by men who put women down with the casual ease that comes from operating in a world where women may be the customers but are rarely the boss.

In the boardroom, it's the usual boring snide asides and power plays. I've actually come to be amused by their predictability. On photoshoots there's an unmistakable hierarchy of power and at the top of it, almost without exception, is the photographer. It's the photographer who calls the shots literally and figuratively: directing the model, the lighting, the overall creative vision. And invariably the photographer is male. The gender dynamic has long been entrenched in the industry, shaping not only who holds authority on set but also how subjects – mainly women – are framed, portrayed and ultimately consumed by the audience.

We're shooting a fashion story for our new Harvey Nichols magazine at a gritty studio in North London. Floor-to-ceiling windows mean the space is flooded with light, but it's also like a greenhouse in there. The poor model in next season's knitwear is sweating, a make-up artist frantically dabbing blotting paper on her forehead in between shots.

The photographer is one of the most in demand of the moment. Not that you'd be able to tell from his baggy, low-slung jeans and dog-eared T-shirt. It's a coup he's agreed to work with us. A sign that the magazine isn't just seen by the industry as advertising for Harvey Nichols, but an editorial product as creative as the *Vogue*s and *Marie Claire*s of the time.

I'd decided to launch our own publication when I realised that instead of having to sweet-talk the editors of those publications to shoot and tell stories about Harvey Nicks, we could do so ourselves. But I knew that it couldn't be some poxy pamphlet that got tossed out with the tissue paper when our customer got her shopping bag home. I wanted a magazine that customers would be proud to leave on their coffee table.

I knew that meant I needed the best magazine brains on it, which is why I'd approached the team at independent publishers Redwood, who'd left legacy media to go out and start their own venture. We recruited Condé Nast's Tina Gaudoin as editor and poached Jason Shulman from the *Telegraph* as creative director – both feisty talents, with short tempers and exacting standards, the classic editorial mix.

I called them my naïve experts: they didn't know my industry, but they knew theirs and vice versa. If we respected each other, then together we could be a powerful force. I loved the push and pull I had with them in editorial meetings, where we'd skip seamlessly around topics – from the genius of Michelle Pfeiffer in *Dangerous Minds* to whether McQueen would join Givenchy – before returning to business: how to bring the story of Harvey Nichols to life on the page.

Today's shoot is designed to do just that. The concept is Unravelled. The model is wearing the best of Antonia's selection of oversized knits, paired with nothing more than knickers, ankle socks and messy hair. We want it to feel candid, like you're capturing the coolest girl you know as she's padding around her boyfriend's house on a Sunday morning.

The model doesn't have to fake that sense of nonchalance. It's a mood that seems to come naturally to the breed of women who go into modelling. I'm yet to be on a shoot where the model doesn't arrive late, say little but turn it on as soon as she's in front of the camera. Maybe the model needs to be calm in the sea of activity that happens around her. Fashion assistants unpack, steam and painstakingly arrange rails of clothes, tables of jewellery – most of which will remain untouched throughout the day. The photographer's assistants tinker constantly: rigging lights, tweaking settings so that the set is just so when the model is finally out of hair and make-up.

I spend most of the day waiting for the shoot to start, bored out of my brain. I feel conspicuous. Not just because my red Norma Kamali shorts and brocade Rifat Ozbek cropped jacket with its burnished gold trim are far smarter than the ubiquitous all-black shoot uniform. I don't like having nothing to do, no set role. I might be the boss in the sense I'll be signing off the final edit of photographs, but at this point there's very little I can do to direct the shoot. I must leave that in the hands of the very famous seventy-year-old photographer who's currently out back having a fag.

Not that I don't try. Hours later, when we've finally started shooting, I'm bending down to tweak a model's socks, when the photographer slaps me on the arse.

'Sexy shorts,' he cackles.

The slap echoes around the cavernous studio but nobody says a word.

Later, the fabulously confident stylist Molly, who has worked with this photographer for years, corners me at the coffee machine and whispers, 'When he next bends over, put your hands around his balls . . . and squeeze.'

The thought of it makes me feel sick, but I do it. It's like cradling a pair of overripe peaches desperately past their sell-by date.

Nailing Barbie to the wall

KEN HAS COMMISSIONED SOME CUSTOMER research he hopes will drive efficiency and help us to increase revenue per customer. I wish I could tell him a more efficient way of understanding our consumer would be to engage with the woman on the shop floor or, better still, his staff. Instead, he thinks that a bunch of American consultants can come up with some game-changing ideas off the back of a tick-box survey. He has always felt the Americans do it better.

'We're a nation with a better work ethic,' he likes to espouse. 'There are more hours in the day than Europeans give days credit for.'

So we've all been summoned to the boardroom to sit through a summary of the consultants' findings. I hope they're considered important enough to merit the lemon shortbread biscuits, at least.

As predicted, the research is uninspiring. The biggest takeaway is the one I've heard from these kinds of people time and time again: we should be targeting the thirty-five-year-old woman, even though we all know most of the spend still comes from the fifty-plus customer. Why is it that everyone always thinks mid-thirties is the ultimate demographic to win over? All I see when I wander through the shop floor are independent, well-dressed older women, many of them businesswomen, with careers and disposable income. They're the ones with their own credit cards and inclination to shop. As I've discovered since having Mylo, women in their thirties are financially crippled by childcare costs, knackered, time-poor and feel shit about their bodies.

I'm still thinking about this as I thumb through the fifty-six-page deck. They want our average customer to be thirty-five – the same age as Barbie. I've just read an article about Mattel's famous doll celebrating her birthday.

An idea starts to form. What if we team up with them for a set of windows that riff on the world's most famous blonde? We can make it kitsch and camp, but it'll also be nostalgic for our customers. Make them fondly remember their youth.

Negotiations with Mattel prove to be extensive and detailed. Faxes from them spiral onto the floor with endless restrictions as to how and what we can do with Barbie's image. But eventually we reach an agreement: we can create a Barbie mannequin and use the dolls to illustrate a window, alongside a 250-piece limited-edition Barbie we'll sell exclusively in Harvey Nichols. We'll dress each of the hundreds of dolls in the window in miniatures of key fashion from the last thirty-five years. Mattel will have to approve every stitch, every inch.

As the seamstresses painstakingly get to work on the dolls' clothes, Donald and I head to Rootstein to ask for Kevin's help shaping a suitably Barbie-curved mannequin. True to form, the showroom is staggering. Harlequin themed, it's entirely black and white, with trapeze-style mannequins and carnival acts dotted amongst them.

'Bit of a palaver, but it's fun, right?' laughs Kevin as Donald wanders around in wonder. Beauty is his drug.

Kevin thinks we should base the Barbie mannequin on one they recently created of the club kid turned fashion muse Dianne Brill. 'Small waist, hourglass figure, pert breasts, platinum-blonde hair,' he says of their mannequin recreation of the woman Andy Warhol christened 'Queen of the Night'. Brill had come into Rootstein's New York studio a few years ago to get her shape immortalised like so many other famous models before her. 'We swept her hair up into a sort of beehive, but we could do it looser for Barbie,' Kevin continues. 'A touch more girl next door.'

He's sketching as he speaks, getting ever more excited by the project. 'What collection is Barbie going to wear?' he asks, sounding like a man Mattel would approve of.

'Our new Harvey Nichols own label. It's fab actually,' I reply.

Jasper Conran and Antonia have been working on the store's first clothing line. We shift so many other designers' clothes, and now we have built Harvey Nichols as a destination and curator of all that's beautiful, the thinking goes, why shouldn't we create our own? The pair have recruited a team to produce a collection of easy-to-wear classics they think every Harvey Nicholas woman wants in her wardrobe: LBDs, a lot of cashmere and sharp suiting.

'OK, how about this?' Kevin says, looking at Jasper's sketches. 'We could riff on the idea of getting Barbie dressed. You could cut some foam board, so they look like those paper clothes we used to cut out of magazines and dress dolls up in. Keep the little white tabs you'd fold over on the sleeves and hems. You choose what she wears!' he continues.

Kevin's passion goes well beyond the scope of what Rootstein is supposed to deliver. But that's exactly why, however much pressure Seb Davey puts on us, I'll never cut our Rootstein budget. They're worth every penny.

As for the outfit for the Harvey Nichols Barbie itself, everyone has an opinion on what she should be wearing.

'Jasper and I were talking, and we think one of the column dresses really would be perfection,' Antonia muses one morning. 'You can't go wrong with a black dress. Timeless.'

'Crystal says it's got to be something pink if we're doing Barbie,' Ken muscles in, reporting back on the conversations he's had with his wife.

It's not worth fighting either of them on this, so we settle on a little black dress worn with an elegant pink silk-collared jacket from the Harvey Nichols own label. Her waist is cinched with a thin patent black belt and she comes with a white chiffon stole with marabou feathers, a leather tote bag and black sunglasses. She's a woman who means business, but also likes to party. Exactly like the woman I think of as our target customer.

Along with 250 limited-edition Harvey Nichols Barbies, boxed and ready to sell to collectors who they warn will flood the store, Mattel also delivers hundreds of naked dolls for the window display. When Des opens the crates, he finds their hair matted, legs akimbo and intertwined. 'I thought you said Barbie is a metaphor for our average customer,' he quips. 'Wonder if this came up in the customer research Ken paid a fortune for?'

The team loses a lot of patience and a few fingernails coiffing and dressing the dolls in the hundreds of outfits the machinists have knocked up for them. Present and correct, it's the Double Ds' job to cover the window's floor and walls with the dolls. They start from the front, twisting, tightening and pinging wire into each doll to get her standing as straight and firm as a full-size mannequin.

'Fuck me,' says Donald. 'We're going be here all night!'

'Right, here's what we'll do,' replies Des, fishing out a hammer from his toolbelt. 'You hold her head and I'll whack a nail in to hold her in place.' On and on they move, hammering the Barbies into the floor and up the wall, until they reach the back row and climb, sweating, out of the window display.

'Always preferred Cindy, myself,' Donald quips, taking a slug of water from his hip flask. At least, I think it's water.

Within a day, the Harvey Nichols Barbie has sold out. Within two days, there are feminist protesters marching up and down Sloane Street. 'Ban Barbie!' their placards read. 'Unrealistic plastic bodies aren't fantastic.' They argue that we're giving a platform to something that perpetuates unrealistic expectations of female bodies, betraying the women who shop at Harvey Nicks. 'If Barbie were an actual woman, she'd be so thin she wouldn't be able to stand up straight, let alone walk or menstruate,' one of the protestors shouts at Harold when he politely but firmly asks them to leave.

Ken's furious, but thankfully not with me. 'What the fuck is this fuss about?' he rails. 'I mean, she's a doll. A doll kids have been playing with for over thirty goddamn years!'

When Bean appears gingerly at my door with a letter that's been delivered, I sense things might be about to shift. A furious ex-customer has issued a fatwa against Harvey Nichols. 'You represent everything that's corrupt about the Western World. You must pay,' they have typed out.

No one is quite sure what to make of it, but the note has freaked Ken out enough to start kicking the shit down the chain.

'Ken wants you to take out the installation, Mary,' Callum reports back. 'He wants it gone by the morning. These are frightening people. We have to take it seriously.'

I spend the night helping the team rip out the Barbies, cursing Des for his nail improvisation. We don't have enough pliers to go around. No one speaks much, and I feel a familiar burn of shame and responsibility.

We've emptied the windows and put back the old 'Pardon our appearance whilst we redress these windows' blind as we try and work out what the hell to do. It gets worse when Bean puts through a telephone call from Anita Roddick. The founder of The Body Shop is a hero of mine. She has managed to create a hugely successful brand that doesn't sell beauty based on that banish-wrinkles bullshit but by making people feel good about the products they buy. The Body Shop campaigns on ending animal testing. It's trying to get people to open their eyes to the destruction of the ozone layer by CFCs. And it makes a mean mango body butter. Anita is a visionary – a woman who inspired and intimidates me in equal measure. She'll go on to launch her own riff on Barbie a few years later: a campaign starring Ruby, a doll proudly showing off her lumps, bumps and size 14 bottom. 'There are 3 billion women who don't look like supermodels and only 8 who do,' is the slogan of the advert that goes on to win every industry award.

'What were you thinking, Mary?' she launches straight in to reprimand me about my Barbie windows. 'You have a responsibility, a platform. Is this really how you want to use it?'

'No, no,' I stumble back, unusually lost for words. 'It was just supposed to be fun . . . A silly, cute bit of fun.'

I'm tormented by the fact that I've fucked up. I spend hours that night saying the same thing over and over to Graham: that I've destroyed a twenty-year career with just one window. There's a widely held truth in the creative industries that you are only as good as your last project. Your most recent work often defines your current value, talent or relevance. His reassurance can't puncture the belief that my reputation looks pretty shaky right now.

'I made you some of my granny's Eccles cakes,' Bean says the next morning, delivering me a basket of pastries. 'She always said they worked wonders with a hot cup of tea.'

Bean believes food cures all ailments. Given how good these are, she's got a point. 'Want one?' I offer her the basket.

'Oh, well, I really shouldn't,' she replies, diving in even as she says it.

As we work our way through the cakes, crumbs and caster sugar littering the sofa, Bean works up the courage to say her piece. 'You know, Mary, you can't blame yourself. Teams are teams, in good and bad. Everyone worked on those windows. No one thought some fundamentalist feminists would threaten to bomb Knightsbridge just because we put a brigade of Barbies in the window. Quite frankly, I thought it'd be more likely we'd get asked where they got their blonde done.'

We both laugh.

'Anyway, everything happens for a reason. We're boxing the Barbies up to send to Great Ormond Street in the morning,' Bean, ever the sage, continues. 'Come help us. The kids won't care about the holes in their feet.'

And as I wrap the Barbie dolls in Harvey Nichols tissue paper, smoothing down their static hair as I go, it strikes me that success doesn't have to be measured by sales revenue and industry acclaim. Retail can be brutal. 'Will it make money?' is the one-liner CEOs are driven by. I know in my heart there's so much more at play. We need to open our eyes to the impact it can make, the joy it can spark – how it brings us together as a team fostering emotion and passion. When we feel excited about an idea, the magic resonates to the customers too. Business, like life, isn't binary and linear. It can be purposeful and profitable. And Anita Roddick is right: I've got a unique opportunity here. I've got to use it. Time to take her out for lunch.

Don't wear an Arabella Pollen jumpsuit on the Eurostar

ANTONIA AND I HAVE EMBARKED on a day trip to Paris to visit some designer showrooms. It's so much easier since Eurostar. It still blows my mind that I can walk onto the train in Waterloo after dropping Mylo at nursery and be having moules frites in Brasserie Lipp by lunch. Though I might stick to salade Niçoise this time – I'm seven months pregnant. This will be my last work trip for a few months.

I'm wearing an Arabella Pollen jumpsuit to try to minimise my bump. I've found the Parisian set frown upon pregnant women almost as much as Harvey Nichols board members. I distinctly get the impression from Ken that my having two kids in quick succession wasn't in his business plan. Despite the fact that I barely took any time off with Mylo and he can hardly say I haven't been as effective ever since being back, he'd been lukewarm when I told him my news.

It was hard not to feel like being pregnant was a weakness

when it was barely mentioned, except in reference to a project I wouldn't be able to see through to the end.

'I just hope your team can keep things on track because we don't want to see budgets spiralling,' Seb would pipe up sanctimoniously during the meetings when he came in for his regular monthly meetings with my department. I'd be desperate to pee but determined to see it through to the end. Exiting early would only give him more ammunition. And I wouldn't be there to defend myself.

By this point I did need to pee constantly. Which is how I found myself squatting with my jumpsuit round my knees so as not to touch the cold metal rim of the Eurostar bog.

The door sounds with a loud beep as it inches open onto the corridor. Fuck, in my haste I mustn't have noticed that there's now a 'close' button and a 'lock' one too. Now it's opening, exposing me mid-stream. I lunge forward, trying to hit the 'lock' button and scramble to pull my jumpsuit that's pooled around the floor back up my legs. As the automatic door inches painfully slowly closed I find myself face to face with Condé Nast's managing director.

Nicholas Coleridge raises one eyebrow and smiles gleefully. 'One for the book, Mary,' he laughs.

Life can be divided in two: before kids and after kids

I DISCOVERED I WAS PREGNANT for the second time on a previous trip to Paris earlier that year. Initially, I'd put my nausea down to four espressos, early starts and the standard lack of food, but the next day I was rational enough to seek out a pharmacy where I could buy a pregnancy test. 'Let me know how it goes,' the elderly French chemist smiled when he handed it over in a discreet brown paper bag.

It's not just the rows of no-nonsense skincare that make French pharmacies a mecca for so many women, it's the service. Like the best retailers, there's a sense of individualism to pharmacies that have often been handed down the generations: the elders teaching new chemists to watch customers carefully, picking up on their unspoken cues, building a relationship of trust. That's what really keeps customers coming back.

Once again, I kept quiet at work about my pregnancy until it was no longer possible to hide my growing belly. This time around,

I didn't just suspect I would be treated differently, I knew it would be the case.

Since having Mylo and returning to work it had become increasingly clear that the workplace was created by men for men. There is only one race. And to win in that race, there is only one lane. Fast, furious and fucking unequal; having a baby wasn't compatible. I can understand how this has happened: most of my mother's generation hadn't worked in corporate environments. We were only really about fifteen years into women working at senior level, and any discussion of showing your true self at work, diversity, equality and any kind of equitable parental support was far in the future.

Besides, the bullish alpha culture had worked for me before. I'd thrived on the pressure. The stakes were high, but so was the heady feeling when you delivered. But since having Mylo I'd started to see how unnecessary so much of the behaviour I saw at work really was. And as soon as I'd opened my eyes to that truth, I couldn't unsee it.

A meeting would suddenly be put in for 8 a.m., with no thought that anyone might need to rearrange childcare. But it was more than just the practicalities. My attitude had shifted. Now, success didn't look like pulling an all-nighter to put together a board presentation fuelled by caffeine and sugar. It meant acing that deck but being home in time for dinner.

As my pregnancy progressed, I was limb-achingly exhausted all the time, juggling looking after a one-year-old with long, intense hours where you'd wrap up one project only for another to begin in parallel. There was no let-up. The pace was relentless.

'I've made you an appointment with Constance,' Bean will tell me from time to time, wrapping a serape around me and ushering me to the basement. The Harvey Nichols nurse was there to keep the hundreds of employees fit and well. It was billed as a benefit, having medical staff on site who could dish out flu jabs and patch up gashes, but I expected Ken kept Constance more to ensure the workforce stayed healthy – and so didn't have a reason to leave work to see their own doctors. Still, I never resent a trip to Constance's office. She knows exactly what I need: a twenty-minute power nap. She'll roll out a fresh strip of white paper, pass me a pillow and disappear for a cup of tea. It's a godsend.

And then my daughter Verity arrives, bang on time early one November morning. Eager and easygoing – a sign of what's to come. It helps that this time around I've hired a maternity nurse, something I've discovered is de rigueur for the staff on *Vogue* who become mothers. They're onto something.

Jo is in her sixties – the age my mother would have been – with two grown-up kids and years of wisdom. Each night, she'll knock gently on my door and lower Verity to me in bed when it's time for a feed. I'll watch Verity suckle and snuggle, awed, once again, at how my body is keeping her alive, before passing her back to Jo who will settle and pat her to sleep. On the odd occasion Mylo also wakes, she'll guide him away from my room and into her own, soothing him with her calm whispers.

I don't need to ask Jo for anything but, instinctively, she knows what I need. The washing is done, neat little babygrows ironed and put away. 'Shall we pop out and get something for dinner?' she'll suggest each afternoon, when she can see we're all getting restless and in need of some fresh air.

It's times like these I'm grateful for my job, for the financial security it provides. I know it's a privilege to be able to afford Jo by my side day and night. Like so many other women in my situation, I might not have my mum to swoop in, but I've worked hard to be able to outsource help to create the stability I now know how much I crave.

I think about what my mother would think now. Would she be proud of me?

I wonder if she ever looked at me all those years ago in all my teenage chaos – the embarrassment I brought her with my school reports, the teachers who despaired, the hopelessness, my anger, all of it . . . I wonder if she ever looked at me and saw beyond it. If, even in the thick of it, she knew that one day I would grow into something more than that reckless, crazy child and saw glimpses of the woman I would become. That I'd step into the same familial role she once filled, holding everything together, making sure everyone was safe and cared for.

God, I understand her now in a way I never did before: the exhaustion, the selflessness, the constant love and vigilance that goes unnoticed. She didn't have any of the luxuries of my life today nor the outside recognition that comes from work. She just loved and delivered. Every single day until she died.

But I know she's with me. I feel her presence in all the ways I instinctively parent my children and create my home. I think she would be happy watching that. I think she would be proud of me now. And with that, suddenly, I feel such extraordinary peace.

In three weeks, Verity is sleeping through the night. One morning, I jolt awake at 6 a.m., my breasts rock solid, realising I haven't done the midnight feed. I've had eight hours' sleep. It's exquisite. I feel like me again. I cry like a baby myself when Jo leaves, her job done. She's done more than establish a solid sleep routine. She loved me, cared for me, did such beautiful, small acts of kindness that a mother – and only a mother – could understand. With Jo by my side, I've enjoyed this newborn stage, realised that being a good mother also meant occasionally being good to myself. I'll forever be grateful to her for that.

The 'have it all' myth

EARLIER THAT YEAR, I'D BEEN headhunted by a famous store chain about a job in New York. I was often being approached about rival roles but this one I took seriously, discussing the merits of living in the Big Apple on a rare family holiday with Graham. While Mylo napped, we sat in the garden of the French farmhouse we'd rented for a week, breaking off hunks of a crusty baguette from the local boulangerie and debating the move. I liked the idea of raising Mylo in a city big on optimism. New York gave me energy. But I knew I would desperately miss my siblings and, as Graham kept reminding me, US companies had an even worse view of maternity leave than in the UK. We both wanted another child. Once again, it didn't feel like the right time to leave.

I had such a privileged life. I'd be flown business class, put up in beautiful hotels and treated to fancy dinners in impossible-to-reserve restaurants. I had a healthy expense account and a store discount. Occasionally, I'd be sent kind gifts from designers or clients. I'd become literate in luxury, able to articulate the advantages of Jil Sander versus Joseph. I appreciated the beauty of the objects I was surrounded by, the feel of lightweight cashmere, the delicious curve of a Conran chair. And I loved the people I got to work with: pioneers who were passionate about culture, food and good conversation.

My mother was a frugal woman. I'd watched her run a household on a tight budget, never wasting food, ironing wrapping paper to be used a second time. As a child I loved tipping out the just-in-case buttons she saved in an old porcelain tobacco jar, sorting them into decorative piles. But while my mum made sure we lived within our means, she never made us feel afraid of money. I don't remember feeling fear of what we couldn't afford. I just knew that my parents were people who had their heads screwed on. When my mum died and my dad abandoned us, their old bank manager took it upon himself to give me and my siblings some advice. 'Don't you go relying on credit cards. Don't buy what you can't afford. If you can't pay off the credit card, don't put it on. It's a slippery slope thereafter,' he'd told us – words that had stuck with me.

I wasn't driven by money, but I liked it. Both for the security it provided and the world it was giving me access to. But occasionally I found myself uncomfortable.

Some friends invited us to their country place for the weekend. Iris was on the display team at Harrods with me years ago but gave up to start a pottery business when she married Richard and had kids. He's in private equity, but I expect his parents gifted him the Suffolk pad, just as they pay for his kids to go to private school. I'm beginning to realise how many school fees are paid by grandparents, who cannily set up trusts at birth. Is it realistic for Graham and me to afford something similar on our salaries? I often wonder.

Verity is only a month old and Mylo is a just-turned two-year-old ball of energy. It was a deliberate decision to try for a second child so quickly. I'd rationalised that it was better to get the disruption – to both life and career – over as swiftly as possible. But a twenty-two-month gap was proving challenging.

I'd watch Mylo hold Verity on the sofa, his little legs not yet long enough to make it over the edge, wanting to be the dutiful big brother. Then he'd get distracted, stand up and Verity would slide off his lap, her little body tilting head down towards the floor as I lunged forward, arms outstretched, with reflexes that would make a goalie proud.

I know it's common for older kids to feel replaced when a baby comes alone. But I feel guilty I've chosen to have such a small age gap. No wonder Mylo doesn't understand why my attention is now split.

I could do with a break, and so I persuade Graham that a weekend with Iris, Richard and their two boys will be fun. And it is. Their place is massive. Iris and I watch as the boys build a bonfire in the garden and toast marshmallows for the kids, who flit between the fire and the swing set. A classic London child, Mylo charges around the garden. He's never seen such open space before.

We're packing up to head back to London on Sunday afternoon, and Richard is closing up the house, putting lights on timers and turning the radiators down so the pipes don't freeze. He'd opened a bottle of Bollinger at lunch, but we'd only drunk a few glasses, and I watch as he drains a good half-bottle down the sink, the bubbles foaming at the plughole. So this is what money does, I think, feeling a deep sense of unease.

Stuck in Sunday-night traffic, the kids are snoozing and the car is blissfully quiet. I find myself wondering what Iris's life would be like if it were mine. Mentally trying it on for size. What would it feel like to have the privilege not to have to work? The financial security to know your house, your family would be fine without you bringing in a wage?

It feels a bit like I've spent my life so far on a treadmill, running, running, running against the clock. I haven't resented that pace. I've wanted it, found satisfaction in the achievement and security it's given me, but now the enforced break of a few months maternity leave has made me press pause. I'm suddenly realising that people around me are doing things at very different paces. That there isn't only one setting: full pelt.

Of course, many of the new mums I'm meeting through soft play and toddler groups look at my life with the same mix of bemusement and wonder as I'm feeling towards Iris. I know I'm privileged. To be able to have a maternity nurse and now a nanny who'll enable me to go back to work. To have a husband who, since he moved from a corporate world into teaching, can be more flexible than most other fathers.

But I don't have the choice to walk away from work. I've put myself in the role of the big earner.

I don't resent Graham for this shift in our financial dynamic. He certainly supported me when I had nothing. Besides, when we made that decision together, I wanted Graham to be happy, for our life to be harmonious.

And, rationally, I know I don't really want to walk away from work. I've learnt that even the toughest times – in life and in business – are the times you grow the most. Pressure turns carbon into diamonds. It's turned me into the woman I am today.

Still, I can tell you whoever came up with three months' maternity leave was certainly not a mother. Even the thought of having to leave Verity in a few weeks' time is enough to make my breasts tingle, my stomach stab. It's my body's involuntary reaction to what feels like pure brutality. But I know I'll have to be tough, to act professional, to park my personal life when I walk through the doors of Harvey Nichols again.

My job then will be to keep men happy at work and keep the harmony at home: juggling, metaphorically and physically, one child constantly hanging off my hip. I read a statistic recently that the happiest people in the UK are single women and married men. The unhappiest? Married women and unmarried men. Go figure, I thought. Whatever way you cut it, it's a lose–lose for women. And I can't see how that is ever going to change.

Women, know your value

WHEN MYLO IS AT NURSERY, I spend most of the time in bed with Verity – luxuriating over every little move she makes. Last time, I'd been so floored by having a newborn, I'd wished the time away – desperate to just make it through each day, for Mylo to feel less fragile and for me to feel more in control again. Now, aware that I'm on borrowed time, I take things at our own pace.

I put *(What's The Story) Morning Glory?* on full blast and laugh as Verity involuntarily bats her arms and legs around – discovering her limbs can move to a backdrop of Oasis. Mylo sitting on his potty one morning just shouted out 'champagne supernova'. Oasis was definitely the soundtrack to my children's childhood, their anthems echoing through the chaos and joy. I sing to Verity, although she's already wide awake. Alert, that word that's only really used with babies. I'm enjoying mothering so much more.

Which makes the idea of returning to work bittersweet.

At least I know enough to throw money at the problem. Going back into the office when my body still feels bruised and my boobs are still leaking will be easier with a wardrobe of ironed shirts, a freezer full of food and the nanny Susannah on standby to do more than a few late nights. I tell myself I'll do anything that will give me a breather. But the transition is still a brutal one, in large part because a few weeks after my return Antonia tells me she's leaving.

'It's time, darling,' she says over a steaming plate of cacio e pepe at Signor Sassi. I'm enjoying eating food while it's still hot. 'I'm leaving this crazy place, I'm leaving the travel, I'm leaving the hours that I spent in my office rather than at home. When I found myself making up a new rule that I could only cry in taxis, it just became untenable,' Antonia confides.

She tells me the place has changed. 'It's a shame,' she laments. Ken had told Antonia she'd have to phase out some of the British designers who were on the slide, out-sexed by the Italian and Parisian names who had bigger marketing spends and a government who believed in the business of fashion. It was Seb's doing, she suspected, coming off the back of one of his spreadsheets analysing revenue per square footage. I understood Seb's decision, but could also appreciate that it wouldn't have been easy for Antonia to oust some of the names she'd brought on board, nurtured and become friends with.

Like a great meal, teams are at their best when there's a perfect alchemy of people – sweet, strong and, yes, a little spicy at times. That's how we were – until Antonia left. Without her delicate, curious mix of old-school elegance and super-cool competitive edge, the balance has shifted. Ken now only has eyes for the big boy consultant. In fact, Seb might as well run the board meetings. Ken asks him to 'kick off' with charts that show month-on-month financial performances. Previously, we'd always started with the best-sellers, new launches and customer and media feedback. Now, each department has its revenue broken down line by line, so we can spend hours discussing why sandals have failed to hit six-figure sales. Anything that can become a metric is codified, and the once vivid canvas of creativity begins to fade. Decisions that once prioritised innovation and risk are now reduced to metrics.

It isn't just that Seb seems to be the kind of financial consultant who enjoys making us squirm as we justify our department's decisions – though he certainly doesn't mind that part. What I've come to realise is that, for him, it is not about what we sell, the product, the store, or even the customers. His focus is purely on efficiency and profitability, nothing more. He could be working with any business, in any industry, and it wouldn't make a difference to him. Luxury doesn't matter – it's all just a numbers game and a series of strategic decisions, and that's the only thing that really interests him.

By contrast, there are many things I appreciate about Callum's leadership. I recognise that it's his trust in me, the space he's given me, that has helped me and the business grow. I know I'm lucky to have had a boss who greets my madcap ideas with a faux-sigh and a grin. 'God, what have you got for me this time, Portas?' is all he'll say. Callum has never tried to suppress me. By contrast, he's let me be me – and then some. That's a wonderful skill in a manager. But sometimes, his non-intervention comes across as nonchalance and that's something I find hard to tolerate.

'You know as well as I do that Seb doesn't get what we're trying to do here,' I argue. 'He doesn't see the value in anything creative, doesn't understand that this is a business about emotional connection – and now I find out he's suggesting cuts to my budgets while adding a number-crunching nerd to Nigel's team. It's an insult.'

I find it hard to tolerate the very British reticence to talk about money. Money matters. There, I said it. And it's not just because I need money to pay the mortgage, the nanny and keep food in the fridge. It's more than just the practical. It's intrinsically linked to value. What you pay someone shows how much you value them in your company. So what does it say that Seb's underlings are being paid as much as me? It's hard not to feel that this place is becoming two camps: oil and water. And we all know how badly those mix.

Yet again, I wolf down a sandwich at my desk. I've still got mountains of work to get through and I know that I'll be in the boardroom for hours. Often the board meetings run into the evenings, at which point, Ken will argue that we may as well go out for a drink. It doesn't matter if one bottle becomes two: these men all have a wife at home. I have a nanny and a frustrated husband. I've lost track of the amount of times I've had to find an excuse to sneak out of the meeting and ask Bean to call home to say I'll miss bedtime – for the third time that week.

All this for a company that seems determined to demonstrate they are fixated on productivity at the cost of creativity, rewarding number-crunching over inventiveness.

The vitality of movements

M Y BEDSIDE TABLE IS GROANING with books I keep meaning to read before bed. One, written by a Franciscan priest from New Mexico who is eyes-open to the faults of the church, really stays with me.

In his book *The Wisdom Pattern*, Father Richard Rohr summarises a pattern of five stages of change that have taken place in religious institutions but that I think also often apply to businesses. He calls these stages 'The Five Ms': human, movement, machine, monument and memory. The thinking goes that many of the great things in history start with a *human*. If a person, or a small group of people, have an idea full of life that reflects a moment or a new way to look at the world, that idea often moves to the second stage of becoming a cultural *movement*. That's the period of greatest energy and vitality. The business these people work in then becomes the vehicle for that movement.

He argues – and I'd agree – that this initial stage is always very exciting, creative and, also, risky. Often, we feel out of control in this stage, and yet it's where we are our most innovative and alive.

But our instinct as humans is to feel safe. So the desire for control moves us as quickly as possible out of and beyond the risky movement stage to the *machine* stage. Where we become mechanical: trying to rinse and repeat the actions that got us this growth in the first place. Automate things. This is predictable and understandable. It is, quite literally, human nature.

But it is also inevitable that the institutional or *machine* stage of a movement will be a less-alive manifestation. This doesn't have to be bad, but it's always surprising for those who see it as an end in itself instead of merely a vehicle for the original vision. When we don't realise a machine's limited capacities, we try to make it into something more than it is. We make it a *monument*, a closed system operating inside its own, often self-serving, logic. By then, it's very hard to take risks, and eventually this monument and its maintenance and self-preservation become ends in themselves.

This is exactly the trap I fear Ken and Seb are leading Harvey Nichols into.

When the company wasn't making any money, risk was permissible – encouraged even. You'll try anything because there's quite literally nothing to lose. But when money starts rolling in – because of the very risks you have taken – the desire for control seeps back in.

In the months ahead, I see this starting to play out at Harvey Nichols.

Ken and co., with their annual bonuses to protect, get more cautious. Board meetings are now about what we took last year, how we're tracking versus forecast, versus plan. We're starting to chase the profit rather than the ideas. I'm beginning to feel that this business I have so loved is losing sight of the innovation that got us this growth in the first place.

Grey Saturdays, Play-Doh and eye bags

I START EVERY WEEKEND DETERMINED to make the most of the kids. Even though I'm not with them enough, they know who their mum is. Their joy when I'm around is infectious.

But it's Saturday morning and the Play-Doh is sludgy brown from being mixed together and if I hear 'Bop It!' one more time I'll scream. It's only ten, I've been up with them since six, and it's raining. The day stretches in front of me with hours that need filling. I love my kids, but I don't love these repetitive, tedious, thankless days.

I haven't found many women with kids in the area who I can be myself with. Many have opted to give up work to stay at home, and it often feels like they can't get comfortable with me when they find out I haven't. There's a curious mix of those who feel judged by my job and those craving excitement, who want to leach it out of me. It's draining.

The only exception is Kate. She arrives for lunch triumphantly wielding a bottle of Le Fat Bastard Chardonnay, a rotund hippopotamus on the label. Who can find the silliest wine has become a running joke. A group of clever wine importers have realised that the new demographic of middle-class female wine drinkers are fed up of Château de Pretentious Merlots, with names we can't pronounce. They think shock-tactic names will help their bottles stand out, and they're right – at least they make Kate and me laugh. Last week, we had Goats Do Roam to celebrate Kate's first book being published. We decide to see how Fat Bastard will measure up – accompanied by the kids' chocolate fingers, a bag of Monster Munch and stories about our week.

It feels good to be myself with Kate. To be able to tell someone how hard I'm finding it all. I'm exhausted. At work, the juggle is batting away bullish board members while energising my team, protecting them from the behaviour above that won't help them do their job, and keeping the creativity going. It's like playing both Cordelia and the Fool in *King Lear*, a dual role that requires energy. Energy I don't have after a weekend trying to pour every ounce that's left of me into the kids. And the 1% that's left into my marriage.

Later that weekend, as I'm getting Mylo's bag ready for nursery, I find an invitation to a ukulele concert I didn't know about and have missed. He won't remember I wasn't there – he's two – but how much longer will that reasoning stack up?

Leed-ing the way

SINCE IT WAS ESTABLISHED AS a linen shop in 1831, there's only ever been one Harvey Nichols. But we're about to change all that. It's the late 90s, and expansion is on everyone's minds – most of all the finance team's. So the decision is made to launch a Harvey Nichols in Leeds, and it's my job to get the world excited about it. Easier said than done for a fickle fashion crowd who are used to Place Vendôme, not West Yorkshire.

We've never worked with advertising agencies before, but the Chairman has increased my budget. It's a big store that's going to need a steady stream of customers to make it a success, and he wants to make a big splash. A clever ad campaign will help: billboards, newspapers, magazines, the lot.

I approach all the top agencies, asking them to come and pitch to win the account. For weeks, my office is a rotation of ad men with egos and blokey ideas. Jesus, it's uninspiring as they take me through endless decks, for which they've killed half a rainforest, to tell me what I already know: the windows are our selling point.

I lose track of the amount of supposedly cutting-edge agencies who include showcasing a live performance in the Leeds windows. It's hard to know if they're complacent or on a killer comedown from the night before.

If I'm being fair, most fashion brands concentrate on the aesthetic. They're less about the act of persuasion, and where they do want to tell their story, they rely on art photography and cinematic visuals. They'd never use regular ad agencies. Instead, the fashion house's Creative Director and his in-house team will collaborate with the gods of photography, Steven Meisel, Mario Testino and Nick Knight, to produce campaigns.

I was looking for a mix of the two. Beautiful, aspirational fashion branding with the quirky, unique edge that gave Harvey Nichols its character. It wasn't an easy task.

The only agency that sparks something in me is an upstart – new and unproven. Sammy and Alan founded their business a few years ago after leaving one of the big agencies. They tell me they'd grown sick of pandering to whichever account holder had the deepest pockets that month. Not least because those were usually the soulless corporates throwing big budgets at ad agencies to solve a problem. The industry's currently abuzz with rumours that utility trade organisations have briefed agencies to work on a campaign repositioning global warming as a theory, not fact.

'We're lucky,' says Sammy, 'but, I'm not going to lie, it's been bloody stressful.'

'The first year was tough,' Alan agrees. 'There were moments where I thought we'd made a huge mistake. Some nights I still don't sleep. You look around at all these people here and realise their livelihoods depend on you keeping the accounts coming in.'

The pair are now working with a range of clients across food, and even London Zoo, but we'd be their first luxury fashion retailer. Plus, I'd hazard a guess, ease their financial pressure. What I loved about them was they listened. They wanted to learn. To understand the world of luxury and where I wanted to take Harvey Nichols. They ask astute questions about our perspective, our attitude, and use the answers to present a series of ideas that aren't quite fashion enough but nonetheless deliver on the irreverence that's come to define us. I can sense their hunger. Not just to win the account, but to understand the luxury market – and then disrupt it.

I get a similar energy exchange from Sammy and Alan as I do the team at Redwood. We'll have difficult meetings, where it's clear they don't understand the emotion of shopping, and I zone out as they try to explain the 4:3 frames needed to plaster around Leeds city centre. We spend months wrestling ideas, adding depth and nuance with each late-night brainstorm. So often now, with my Harvey Nichols team, they would look to me to tell them what we were doing that day. Working with contemporaries, equally as driven as me but with a different field of vision, was far more combative but also more invigorating. I was learning as much as directing.

Where we eventually land feels good. We decide we'll shoot a monochromatic fashion story but with the model wearing a bright pink dog collar around her neck.

'And for the tagline we're thinking: Harvey Nichols Leeds (Not Follows),' I tell Callum as we're in the lift on the way to the boardroom.

He likes it. It's slick but edgy. It'll help us get premium front-half positioning in *GQ* and British *Vogue* and no doubt leave those *Telegraph* weekend readers spluttering out their English Breakfast tea. We want this launch to be splashy and noticeable. This campaign delivers.

Like any good idea, once it's out there it gains momentum. Stylists, photographers, casting agents, set-builders and the rest of the huge team of creatives who work on pre-production add their own flair to deliver pictures that can hold billboards and banner ads. Casting Jodie Kidd is a coup. The English model has become a favourite of Chanel designer Karl Lagerfeld: rumour is he's about to put her on an exclusive contract, meaning she won't be able to work with anyone else. But Jodie's a Harvey Nicks customer: she's always popping in for a miniskirt or some MAC eyeliner.

On set, Jodie is full of stories of the week she's just spent with Karl, where he sketches constantly throughout every meal, every conversation designing the perfect dress for her body. You can see why Karl is obsessed with her. When Jodie steps onto set she's hypnotic. You can have the best photographer and all the elements in place, but I still believe it's the model who makes the pictures. Her energy sells the clothes, the idea.

In parallel, Rita has been negotiating with Network Rail to hire a train to take the UK press to Leeds to cover the opening. Her winning combination of bolshiness and charm has seen them agree to give us free rein to decorate one of their trains. But it still has to leave from Euston, London's dingiest train station. We'll need to think carefully about how we bring some glamour to the soulless 60s concrete box, let alone the LNER train itself.

'The MAC boys are working with k.d. lang now,' suggests Des as we're compiling the guest list. 'Why don't you see if they'll fly her over?' Rita's in favour, agreeing that the Canadian singer will add some newsworthiness to the occasion. Notorious for not wearing make-up, k.d. was a surprising choice to take over from RuPaul as the new face of MAC's Viva Glam range. Country music isn't usually my thing, but I love k.d. It's impossible not to croon along to 'Constant Craving', and I was impressed by her attitude to the grief she got from the country music community when she came out as a lesbian. When you go from facing down a picket line at the Grammys and having several American country stations refusing to play your music to appearing on the cover of *Vanity Fair* being given a close shave by a swimsuit-clad Cindy Crawford . . . Well, that's a woman I want to meet. So I make the call to ask the Franks to get on board, quite literally.

There's something so satisfying about seeing an event you've planned for months take shape. The British fashion press are tottering along the corridors of the train to find their seats. Jessica had the clever thought of putting a Harvey Nicks hamper on each seat. It disguises the tattered, stained checkerboard wool fabric, and we're hoping the mini champagne inside will loosen the mood. By the time the train pulls out of the platform – amazingly for

British Rail, bang on time – the corks have been popped and the bubbles are flowing.

I'm sitting with MAC's Frank Toskan and k.d., who is both gentle and funny. She's so at ease. 'I'm a non–lipstick lesbian,' she laughs, talking to a journalist from the *Guardian* about how her collaboration with the MAC team came about. 'I have pretty thin lips, so when people put lipstick on me I look like a drag queen. Not that that would be a bad thing. Still, signing up a singer who doesn't wear make-up as the face of a cosmetics brand? That was a ballsy move.'

If k.d. says she doesn't know why MAC wanted her, she's clear on why she wanted to be involved. It's the Franks' commitment to raising funds and awareness for the AIDS crisis as well as their ethics around animal testing and recycling. 'They're a very Canadian company,' she finishes, 'who have thankfully found a global platform.'

I'm reminded how lucky I am to have worked with the MAC team. It's rewarding when you collaborate with people you respect, people you can learn from. Even better if it's also fun.

I'm grateful for that when we get off the train and cross into New Station Street, where the doors of the new Harvey Nichols are about to open. As I see queues of customers dressed up as Patsy and Edina, I'm also grateful that most of the British press are already *Ab Fab*-level pissed.

The Leeds launch has been a success: customers are flocking there, and Seb's reports show they're buying a very different type of product. In London it's the edgy Ann Demeulemeester and

Dries Van Noten; in Leeds the customer wants the household names, the Guccis and Calvin Kleins.

'And so, as you can see in the numbers, it's a successful example of business diversification,' Ken has started parroting ad nauseam.

His sheen disappears when we're hit with the news that hundreds of people have complained to the Advertising Standards Authority about the Leeds Not Follows campaign. They say that images of a woman wearing a dog collar are misogynistic. That they glamorise domestic violence.

'What a load of bollocks' is Des's sophisticated response. 'Why do people have to take everything so fucking seriously these days? It's like the world's had a collective sense of humour failure.'

Ken's determined to fight the ASA and instructs me to work with our advertising agency on, as he puts it, 'a robust defence'. What that really means is a lot of late nights with the legal team.

I know I should probably be as outraged as Des and the rest of my team. But the truth is that I don't have the energy to be. I spend so much of my day managing the mundane, keeping everything on track and myself afloat. The creative stuff is supposed to be the fun bit, the buzz that makes it all worthwhile. Instead, even that increasingly feels like a struggle. We win the ASA appeal. But I can't shake my feeling of flatness. There's no doubt that doing what we do is now harder, less fun and more churn than creative spark.

Things can only get better

'LONDON SWINGS AGAIN': *VANITY FAIR* have published a cover with Patsy Kensit and Liam Gallagher in bed, partially covered by a Union Jack bedspread. Cass loves it. Ken reminds us that the cover hasn't been printed in the US. Just in case we were getting ahead of ourselves, and believing the notion that British culture was setting the global agenda. But even Ken can't piss on the excitement on Thursday 1 May 1997. We're on the eve of the first Labour government in nearly twenty-three years.

I'm spending election night at Kate's house around the corner from ours. Her husband Martin is one of those brilliant people who lives by his political beliefs. He's a fierce Labour man as well as a celebrated headmaster who has turned around a number of state schools. I've never liked the singular words Ofsted use to rate schools. But Martin's have gone from poor to outstanding.

All the theatre lot are at Kate's, crammed around the TV. The atmosphere is feverish. At 3.01 a.m., when Michael Portillo loses his seat, the place explodes. We'd forgotten Kate's three kids and my two are asleep upstairs until they emerge at the bottom of the stairs, bleary-eyed in their PJs, come to see what all the noise is about. As Graham and I walk home, pushing Mylo and Verity in twin buggies, my slip dress sticking to my clammy legs, I feel giddy. Tony Blair has won.

It's not just that Blair is a Labour prime minister. He's so young, so normal. With her quaffed hair and Launer handbag, Thatcher felt like a woman of another era. At forty-three, Blair could be my big brother. In fact, over the last few months he's often popped into Michael's restaurant, which is a few streets from his campaign office. He takes his tie off, orders a glass of red wine; apparently he looks knackered but buoyant. It's impossible not to share that buoyancy. Blair listens to Oasis. He wants Vivienne Westwood to come to Downing Street. He's not some Eton-educated posho. It feels like someone of our generation, someone who gets us, has come to power. Maybe, just maybe, without such an obvious class and age division, Blair will get the shit done that matters to us.

And if Blair can do the unthinkable – revolutionise Labour and sweep to power – maybe we can all do that too. One of my favourite authors Krista Tippett says hope is a muscle, a practice that propels us forward. That's how it feels. Change is in the air. It's tempting to buy into D:Ream's message that 'things can only get better'.

Life is short

THE MORNING OF SUNDAY 31 August 1997, I am supposed to be taking Mylo and Verity to the playground with Kate and her kids. Instead, we wake to the news that Princess Diana has died.

A long-standing customer of Harvey Nichols, I'd often seen Diana on the shop floor seeking out a Joseph blazer or a pair of white Levi's. I'd heard the story of her first visit after her divorce when the shop assistant had printed off an invoice ready to send to Kensington Palace as per usual, but Diana had whipped out a credit card. 'It's on me! I'm free . . .' she'd said, grinning that famous smile.

Utterly charming, Diana always left you feeling light somehow – even when she was chastising you. I'd been at the Caprice having lunch with Alex Shulman one Wednesday, when a turquoise-suited Diana sidled over and pulled up a chair to join us. She wasn't happy about something or other that had appeared in the pages of British *Vogue* and gave Alex a hard time, but gently, teasing her almost.

It feels impossible that she is gone. The office is eerily quiet for a Monday morning. Antonella's office door is closed, her PA just shaking her head to dismiss anyone who gets close. Bean is so absorbed in the newspaper tributes she's reading at her desk, she doesn't notice me approaching.

'Good morning,' I say, hesitating before interrupting her private grief. 'It's just so awful.'

As Bean looks up at me, her face just crumples. She rescues a hankie with her family insignia stitched in the corner from up her sleeve and sniffs. It's going to be an odd day. No meeting really gets going; everyone is shell-shocked. So I decide to take a break and walk through the park to Kensington Palace. I smell the flowers that have been laid in tribute before I see them: mounds as deep as my knees fanning out against the ornate gates. An industrious *Evening Standard* seller has positioned his stall just by the entrance to the park. 'SATURDAY AT THE ABBEY,' shouts the headline, with details of the funeral procession route alongside a picture of Diana in her powder-pink Versace jacket. She's doing her classic chin down, eyes up look. She looks so alive.

Days later I watch her funeral, clutching Verity close and sobbing. The BBC opens its coverage with Mario Testino's black-and-white image of her with the dates 1961–1997. She was my age. Kate and I have agreed to meet on the Finchley Road to watch Diana's coffin be driven to her family home in Althorp. It feels important to us both to pay our respects, to be part of history.

With Verity strapped to me in a baby carrier, I'm gripping Mylo's hand. He can hardly see a thing; the crowd is twenty-deep. Despite the numbers, there's a sombre silence, broken only by the odd call. 'We love you, Diana!' someone shouts. 'Go safely,' another whispers as her funeral car rolls past, a police escort leading the way.

'Coffee?' Kate asks as we make our way back to the tube.

'Wine,' I reply, and we dive into the first place we see.

The kids scrabble around, making up a game with sugar lumps and paper napkins, as Kate and I try to unpick the emotions around what we've just witnessed.

'I've been thinking about leaving Harvey Nicks,' I say, suddenly vocalising something that's been whirling around my brain for months but today feels urgent. Life is short – and precious.

'I knew there was something going on with you,' Kate answers, 'but I've got to admit I wasn't expecting that.' Instinctively, Kate knows I've not been in a great space. It's felt like there's a heavy weight around me lately. Tensions are high between me and Graham. Two kids in quick succession isn't easy on any marriage, but increasingly it feels like we're on different paths. He's nervous about the idea of me leaving a secure, well-paid job, doesn't understand why I would throw away years of hard-earned career progression. I get it. Graham's always been rational, analytical, cautious – strengths I valued after my childhood. I know I'm impulsive and I can see that my behaviour seems irrational to him, that it's discombobulating. Because in many ways it doesn't make sense. We're comfortable and, on the surface, our carefully orchestrated lives are working. 'Why risk that now?' I can almost hear him thinking.

287

I've never felt uninhibited by change. Sometimes my tendency to throw my cards up in the air and see where they land isn't helpful, but I do also think that instinctiveness is the reason I've ended up here in the first place. I know I have to trust this feeling.

'It's probably madness, but the feeling of wanting something more just won't leave me,' I explain. 'It's too hard a job not to love it, to really want it. I just keep thinking there's so much more out there I could be doing. And I'd be doing it for myself, on my own terms. I can't help but want to try. But maybe Graham's right and it's only when I quit that I'll realise just how good I've had it?'

'Listen, Mary.' Kate looks at me seriously. 'If there's one thing I know about you, it's this. When you've made up your mind, it's happening. It's just a matter of when. It's visceral with you. You're always about moving forwards, but is this the best time right now?'

Kate has always believed in my instincts and ideas. She has faith in me. But she'll also tell me how it is. 'If you really think it is, you should do it. I will say this though: it's not going to be easy,' she continues, extracting a sugar cube from her son's stealthy fingers. 'You'll be starting again. Don't underestimate the impact that'll have on you and the kids. And Graham . . .'

'I know,' I sigh. I am aware I'm not one for planning out every detail meticulously. I'm a feeler more than a thinker. And that is a worry. But Kate is also right about my relentless pace forward: staying static has never been an option for me. I can do some things in haste, but my instinct has served me well so far. I have to listen to that. I know I'm at my peak, and therefore my reputation will be able to get me work, good work. But, equally, I know that this industry is fucking fickle. Right now, I'm Mary Portas at Harvey Nichols. When I'm just Mary Portas, what will the world of work look like?

'And one last thing: as much as I love you, don't think I'll automatically be on hand to help with the kids. It's hard enough fucking dealing with my own.' She pours us another glass of wine.

One last window

I F THESE WILL BE MY last windows for Harvey Nicks, I want to make them really sing. I want to come up with my most audaciously creative brief yet. I want that sense of risk that always sweetens the reward. But, really, I wanted to end with something jaw-droppingly beautiful.

I'd heard about a young artist called Thomas Heatherwick from Terence Conran, a visionary with exceptional taste who quite literally changed the way we all live. How we see and furnish our homes, and how we eat out and entertain. My idea of heaven is wandering through the perfectly curated Conran Store he has just opened at the bottom end of Marylebone High Street. It's impossible to leave empty-handed.

So I'm naturally curious about the artist Terence has been mentoring. 'This young man is a genius,' he tells me one day over lunch at Orrery, recalling how a student Heatherwick chased him down a fire escape after he'd given a talk at the Royal College of Art. 'You must come and see what he's done for me in the store.'

290

I ask for Heatherwick's number and call him with an offer: it's my last window at Harvey Nicks and I want to go out with a bloody great splash. Would he want to do this with me?

We arrange for him to come into Harvey Nichols to see the space for himself and talk through some initial ideas. I know he's only a few years out of the RCA, but I'm still surprised by the scrappy boy who arrives. Messy ringlets of hair hang over his eyes as he shakes my hand and says hello, barely able to look up at me. Then there's the fact that he's brought his mum along with him. Even the usually guileless Bean can't resist a quick raise of her eyebrows as she brings us a pot of coffee.

But as Thomas starts to talk about his ideas, he begins to open up.

'I know usually you treat each window as its own entity,' he starts, 'but I loved it when you created your fish windows on Sloane and made a seamless installation that looked like one continuous piece. I would love to go even bigger and use the whole front run as one huge collective space. Not just ignoring the divisions between each window but the divisions between glass and pavement. Treating the whole shop's façade as the landscape, if you see what I mean? I think that'll give you the scale you're looking for.'

He opens a ring binder, pulling out sketches from the plastic folders clipped in. 'We can make it look like there's no glass in the window,' he pitches. 'And then build a vast wooden branch that snakes through each window and onto the street, weaving in between the pillars of the building.'

'It's a beautiful idea,' I reply. 'But that's some big beast to get right.'

My head has gone straight into what can go wrong after years of doing crazy, ambitious installations that required my builders to construct serious architectural engineering systems to hold them up. 'Can the window frames hold that kind of weight? I'm going to have to rely on your team to scope the logistics.'

Thomas works through my concerns methodically and concisely. Yes, it's a feat of architectural engineering, he agrees, but he believes it can be done. He'll build the individual pieces in a warehouse off site. He estimates it'll take weeks in situ to reconstruct them safely. It feels good to be creatively sparring with him. I can feel his hunger, his ambition. This will be his first public commission; I know he wants the platform, but I can also sense he's scoping me out to see if I'll allow him the freedom to do something that gets him equally excited. I am. But I'm also scoping him out to make sure my graceful final swan song doesn't end up a goose honk.

'OK, let's do it,' I conclude. 'This is going to be fun.' I hold up my coffee cup for an impromptu cheers. 'Next steps, proper scaled drawings. Our carpenter can help with those. And then we'll need legal to draw up a contract.'

'We've made a start on that actually,' pipes up Thomas's mum. She's been quiet to this point, but it now becomes clear why she's here. 'We'll need to agree terms, so we've put together some numbers on what Thomas and his team would require, in order to take this on.' She hands me a spreadsheet with a line-by-line breakdown of the project's proposed costs. I scan down, looking for that final sum. It's a punchy number, far more than I'm used to paying designers with many more years' experience. It'll also bust the budgets for that quarter.

I can't help but laugh. 'Well, there's no flies on you,' I respond, looking at Thomas rather than this mum.

He shrugs his shoulders slightly. 'I really want this, Mary. And I'll work bloody hard. It'll be brilliant,' he says, holding my gaze the entire time.

This is no teenage boy. He's got balls of steel. Which is good to see because he'll need them if he's to pull off what he's suggested.

'We're in,' I reply.

For the next few weeks, I enjoy popping into Heatherwick's studio to see the structures take shape. Floor-to-ceiling windows flood the cavernous space with light as our teams construct the huge, white plywood structures, piecing individual pieces together to create a twisted, curved shape. Des has to stand on a chair to scrawl instructions onto the pieces with the pencil he pulls from his beard. Numbers signify which window the structure will be placed in, triangles and lines the marks that show where new pieces will extend from. It looks like the Natural History Museum's entrance way after a new discovery of dinosaur bones; just like their archaeologists will piece together a T. Rex skeleton, these architects will rig up a sculpture that will weave in and out of the eleven windows and over the frame of the door looking onto Knightsbridge.

Back at HQ, I head up to our Harvey Nichols studio to discuss with Donald the plan for the mannequins. My instinct is to keep it simple: one in each window, wearing pared-back designs from the autumn/winter collections. This display is to celebrate London Fashion Week's talent, but in truth it's more about the art we're creating than selling another frock or two.

'Give us the weeding job, will you?' I hear Cass pleading. That means she's hungover and wants the task that mainly requires lying on the floor and picking off the old staples from the wall panels of vinyl we reuse time and time again. It's a brain-free kind of job.

They've infuriated me at times, but it'll be hard to leave this team behind. They've taught me a lot: about the business of executing brilliant ideas, but also about myself. That I need people around me who challenge and inspire me. People I actually want to be around. But there's also some satisfaction in knowing that just as Kate's reassured me I'll be fine striking out on my own, so will my team. At their best, they're at the top of their game.

I'm sad Antonia is no longer with us to witness the installation of what Heatherwick has christened 'Autumn Intrusion'. It's classy and bold. The rigging team sweat and swear, but miraculously, the anatomical sketches, the 3D models and the pencil marks have done their job. The pieces twist in and out of the panes of glass as if a tree has sprouted out of Harvey Nichols. It's surreal. Beautiful. Quite literally a piece of art.

'I've got to admit, Mary, I wasn't sure about this one,' Ken greets me as we head out for our customary window walk. 'I tried to explain it to Crystal using the girls' Lego and we just couldn't wrap our heads around it. But I'll tell you what, seeing it now? It really is something.'

He's right. There's an electricity as we cross the road to stand outside the Hyde Park Hotel so we can really take in the full scope of the giant sculpture.

'I don't really understand it,' he continues. 'But I'm proud that we've done this.'

For once, Ken and I are in sync.

Punters loved the art bursting out of the windows and above the pavements. The council less so. Clipboard-wielding officials from the Royal Borough of Kensington and Chelsea don't wait long before coming to shut us down. Some old trout who had a permanent suite in the Hyde Park Hotel has complained about its safety. The project has cost us tens of thousands of pounds and, I argue, is a piece of art. Besides, it'll only be up for thirty-eight days. But they are unmoved. It takes Ken calling a friend of a friend high up in the council for them to back off, and even I have to grudgingly admit there are some advantages to the old boys' network.

How do you know when it's time to go?

WE'VE ALL HEARD THAT CLICHÉ that we should follow our passions. But I prefer the author and thinker Elizabeth Gilbert's philosophy that it's our curiosity we should listen to. She argues that so many people suppress their curiosity with reason and logic, but that if you really tune into that curiosity, that's when things start to feel right. When life gets interesting – and carries on being creative.

Whether it's relationships or work, there's never just one reason why people leave. But my curiosity was a big part of why I decided to walk away from Harvey Nichols. I had helped build the business into a globally recognised cultural cornerstone, as well as a profitable retailer. I executed big idea after big idea: show-stopping windows. *Ab Fab*. New Gen. Global first launches. A luxury magazine. Yes, I can continue to think of outlandish, emotional ideas to keep this business top of mind, but something in me has shifted. And I can't unshift it.

Yet it's a tough decision to walk away from a job that I have absolutely loved. A job that in some ways gave me my sense of self and allowed me to bloom. And one I'm getting well paid to do. Especially given I'm the main breadwinner and my kids are still small.

Strangely though, it was becoming a mother that made me start to see things differently. For the first time, I fully understood that responsibility wasn't just about providing for my children – it was also about allowing them to have the confidence to be themselves, to follow their own rhythm and not to have to conform to someone else's expectations of what good enough is.

For so long I had relied on fitting into external structures for a sense of safety, believing that my sense of worth depended on achieving success within those systems. It wasn't Harvey Nichols' fault. It's just the way the world works. There's a boss, a hierarchy, a way of operating. You report to someone, you follow the rules, you learn what 'good' looks like within that framework and you shape yourself to fit it. That's just business. But now I've realised I can't do it any more. Not because it was wrong, but because it is no longer right for me.

Going it alone – truly alone – will mean finally being able to make decisions on my terms. Decisions as simple yet profound as choosing to be there for my children's sports day without needing permission, or deciding to do an interview with a magazine without having to run it past the MD to make sure I won't say anything out of order. The truth is, I like being out of order. I am an out of order person – and I'm finally accepting that. I need to go and do my own thing, in my own way. Whatever the world has in store for me, whatever is waiting beyond Harvey Nichols, I know I have to go and find it.

Kate used to joke that if I had a theme tune, it would be U2's 'I Still Haven't Found What I'm Looking For'. As always, she had it right. I'd often been approached by other companies looking for me to help take them on a similar path of transformation as I had Harvey Nichols. God, no, I don't want to work for *you*, I'd think. Now another thought follows: 'But I would love to get my hands on you.' An idea starts to crystallise: I could launch a creative agency that replicates what I've done for Harvey Nichols.

I realise that so much of my success has been because of a beautiful alchemy of creatives. It was about artists and stylists with big ideas but also precise concepts: the tone of the lighting, the font on a shopping bag, the seat fabric in a fitting room. Craftspeople took that vision and turned it into something 3D – something alive – with inventive window displays. Publicists found new ways to connect these ideas to the public or with journalists, whose mastery of words gave them a language, a purpose. Alchemy is a seemingly magical process of transformation, creation or combination. And while it did feel magical, I had enough confidence now to know that this process wasn't some random mix, it was a performance I led the team through. If they were an orchestra, I was the conductor: no one section was stronger than the other, just as no product, partnership, campaign or window could live in isolation. It was about dialling them up in a frequency that made our audience feel part of something. We gave Harvey Nichols an identity, transformed it into a destination. And made it not just the place to be, but a profitable, dynamic business.

So much of creativity is sidelined by businesses as a 'nice to have' rather than something essential. But when it's properly recognised and embedded into the fabric of the company, it's those creative ideas that drive growth. You cannot remain profitable without innovation. And you can't generate innovation without creative energy.

If I could do that for Harvey Nicks, I could bring that creative direction to other brands too. And, because it'd be my own thing, I'd be able to create my own environment, culture, space and place. My own modus of working.

Part of what I'd always craved from work was stability: an anchor, financially and emotionally, in a world where I operated solo. Now I've achieved that. I've made a name for myself in a notoriously fickle industry. I've got the car, the awards, the wardrobe, the respect. I have finally reached a place of safety. But in doing so, I've also learnt that security doesn't come from a payslip or a team of people around you. It doesn't come from family or a spouse – though they can help, of course. It comes from me. From deep within me. I can do this. I'd started from nothing before. I can do it again.

As I walk into Ken's office, resignation letter in hand, I'm reminded of a Christopher Logue poem my drama teacher used to recite to calm my nerves before my drama school auditions.

Come to the edge.
We might fall.
Come to the edge.
It's too high!
COME TO THE EDGE!
And they came,
and he pushed,
and they flew.

Afterword

A letter to then and now

I'M NOT USUALLY SOMEONE WHO indulges in nostalgia. My pace, my pursuit of the new and the next, has always been both my power and a curse. But writing this book hasn't just been a fun jaunt through the hedonistic binge years of the 90s: it reminded me of how beautifully innovative many of those years were despite often being constrained by outdated norms and limited perspectives.

For a book that's rooted so much in the past, it might seem strange that my instinct today is to say we should leave most of it behind. Nostalgia is a double-edged sword. Extracting the essence of the past and getting inspired by it can propel us beautifully forward, but getting trapped in it can lead us to atrophy, make us reluctant to embrace new possibilities. 'Life can only be understood backwards, but it must be lived forwards,' as the Danish philosopher Søren Kierkegaard puts it. So why don't we do just that?

I joined Harvey Nichols, aged twenty-eight, in 1989: a year that was ripe with significance. The Berlin Wall fell. Thatcher was about to be toppled. Soul II Soul's 'Back to Life' hit the top of the charts. Change was in the air.

But there was something else too. A defiance. A sense that progress was hurtling forwards like a rollercoaster, and it was up to you to jump on board and steer the route.

I'll never forget seeing Jeff Widener's extraordinary photo of the unknown Tank Man in Tiananmen Square that year. The sight of a solitary Chinese protester standing in the way of a column of tanks, plastic shopping bag in hand, is one that still hangs on students' bedroom walls for good reason. We need that defiance – that urge to stand up and make a statement, be part of something – today more than ever.

The world is in crisis. Economies are crashing, politics is toxic, people are divided. As we fight against each other and fight to survive, the world, literally, is burning.

It feels like a pivotal moment, from where we can go one of two ways: we can continue the course of unchecked rampant capitalism, letting the don't-give-a-fuck tech bros run riot. They'll destroy our planet but make the rich richer in the process. Or we can build something new. Something beautiful. Where ideas are guided by imagination and morality. Where success is measured not only in profit but in the richness of culture, the health of communities and the wellbeing of our planet.

Krista Tippett who hosts the wise podcast *On Being*, which I often listen to for inspiration and hope, writes so powerfully about the possibilities: 'This is an age of devastating tumult. It is an age of magnificent possibility. Much is breaking. Much is being born. The two go hand in hand, and that is one of the deepest and strangest, most terrible and most redemptive truths of human reality.' Crisis does force change. I believe that deeply. It clears the way for renewal, for new ideas; movements and possibilities emerge.

As interconnected individuals, we have the power to create change. We each have a role to play – collective action starts with us. But while individual actions can drive progress, the greatest impact comes from the world of business. The way businesses produce, sell and operate has the power to shape our environment, our health, our daily lives and the sustainability of our precious planet.

In the years since Harvey Nichols, I've had the space to reflect on the impact of those years. We were shaping culture, pushing boundaries and creating experiences that were magnetic. Retail was alive with possibility – bold, theatrical and full of joy. But we weren't aware of the impact it was having on our planet. Now we are. So how do we move forward?

I Shop Therefore I Am was artist Barbara Kruger's critical commentary on consumerism in the 90s, a statement about how we often defined our identity through the stuff we bought. I believe that the creative challenge of our time is to powerfully reframe those hollow consumerist years – making 'I Shop Therefore I Am' a conscious choice that is an assertion of agency, responsibility, creativity and hope. To keep that electric, imaginative 90s way of shopping alive but choose to buy from businesses that respect the Earth and are in touch with what truly matters.

Multiple times a day, every one of us makes a decision about what we spend our money on. When businesses make that easy and rewarding for us, it drives change at scale and makes our choices joyful and generative.

I shop, therefore I am investing in the future.

I shop, therefore I am supporting a brand that does its bit to support the planet.

I shop, therefore I am making sure our high street and local communities don't disappear.

I shop, therefore I am saying something about who I am.

So let's get inspired. Let's reimagine retail as an act of storytelling and connection, not just transaction. Where businesses are places of human engagement, where products carry meaning and where creativity isn't sidelined.

A few years ago, me and my team at Portas started wrestling with this question. How can we help brands and companies shift from models of extraction and growth to what we call being 'in the business of beautiful business'? Because one thing I've learnt through my career is this: beautiful business, when done well, is a powerful space for change because it sits at the intersection of commerce and culture.

It's an ever-evolving process. We don't pretend to have all the answers, but there are certain fundamental truths that we are sure of – principles that draw from the past and become the beating heart of the future we are building.

1. Beautiful business is a creative act

Above all else, we have learnt that true creativity, like true progress, is fluid. It moves, shifts and grows in rhythm with the world it is part of. But businesses must find a way to harness it.

Why is it, I ask myself, that so often the role of creativity is diminished? In every corner of the corporate world that I have worked in, creative people – designers, writers, strategists, visionaries – must eventually present their work to someone in finance, or legal, or operations. Their ideas, often born from intuition, emotion, risk and wonder, must be held up to the fluorescent light of reason. They are judged, analysed, signed off – if deemed acceptable.

But in all the years I've worked in business, I've never once seen it happen the other way around. No spreadsheet, no budget forecast, no quarterly projection is ever brought before the creative department for blessing. There is no moment when finance tiptoes into the studio and says, 'Does this feel right to you?' Legal doesn't hand over a contract and ask, 'Is this imaginative enough?' The flow of judgment is one-directional. A one-way mirror. Creatives are seen, assessed – but rarely invited to see back.

What does that say about the value we place on creativity in business?

It reveals a profound imbalance. In most business cultures, creativity is treated as an accessory – something decorative, to be 'added in' once the serious work is done. Never the core, always the fringe. And because creative work often resists quantification, it is placed on trial more frequently, and more harshly, than any metric-driven discipline.

There is, underneath this, a fundamental discomfort: creativity traffics in ambiguity, while business is built on the illusion of certainty. Yet it is precisely in ambiguity that the future lies. Certainty clings to what already exists; creativity imagines what could be.

The companies that will define the next era aren't the ones who merely tolerate creativity. They're the ones who invite it in as a strategic partner, who turn the one-way mirror into a round table. Where finance learns to see with feeling, and creatives are empowered to lead – not just decorate.

The success of Harvey Nichols in the 90s showed that business and creativity can't be divorced – that business at its core is itself a creative act. Retail at its best is a living, breathing connection between ideas and people. A beautiful act of risk and vision distilled into experiences, products and interactions that magnetise people to your brand.

Still, we so often lose sight of creativity and fall into operational mode. When that happens, the heartbeat of business slows to a mechanical pulse of logistics and incremental improvements. We've seen so many retailers that function but don't inspire, selling stuff in volume that lacks joy and desire – existing but not truly loved. Running shops but not serving people.

The problem for these kinds of businesses arrives when they reach a so-called 'good' level of profitability; they cling to it. They become fixed on maintaining margins rather than innovating and pushing forward. Instead of looking ahead to the unmet needs of people and planet, they obsess over the rear-view mirror. It becomes about chasing incremental growth on last year's numbers, growing like-for-like sales, poring over great ideas and putting them through the corporate sieve – analysing them to within an inch of their data-driven lives or consigning them to the advertising fringes.

This is how brands become irrelevant. Worse, they stop adding value to the world. Not in one dramatic moment but gradually, through a thousand safe choices. Data has become the great arbiter. But while it has its place, it cannot replace vision. Progress does not come from mere efficiencies but from leaps of imagination.

So much of what I do with my team at Portas isn't just creating those leaps; it's helping our partners actually make them happen in companies that have been hardwired to only ever do the same. It's our job to help them think and act differently.

As the educationalist Ken Robinson said: 'Creativity is the process of having original ideas that have value.'

Every breakthrough I've ever witnessed in business from the smallest improvement to the biggest game-changing innovation starts with an idea. It's a fundamental truth. An original thought really does have value.

2. Business should be generative not extractive

Every time I'm invited to speak, whether to retail businesses, insurance companies, banks or universities, there's always a moment when someone asks the same question: what are some examples of businesses innovating successfully? What they are really asking is: show me who is nailing it and making good profits so I can ape them.

I understand why they want to know, but I always try to explain that we are in uncharted territory. There are no elders who can guide us into the future, no precedent for this exact moment, no perfect model. Because never before, in any of our lifetimes, have we had to navigate the urgent reality of looking after Mother Earth while simultaneously reimagining business models from the ground up. All of this is emergent, relying on your best first move, one after another.

If I do cite one example, it's always Anita Roddick. Because, if anyone were creating a beauty company today – a truly forward-thinking, ethical and profitable one – they would follow the blueprint the Body Shop founder Anita Roddick laid down in the 70s. The Body Shop wasn't just a beauty brand, it was a global movement and one of the most profitable retail businesses of its time. And at the heart of everything she built was a simple but radical principle: do no harm.

She created supply chains that supported communities rather than exploited them. She rejected animal testing long before it became a mainstream conversation. She refused the artificial, the chemical-laden, the wasteful. And beyond that, she didn't just sell products – she built activism into the very DNA of her business. Her campaigns weren't passive: they were action-driven, punk spiritualist calls to make the world better.

Think about the outpouring of emotion when news broke in 2024 that The Body Shop was going into administration following years of slow dilution by the big conglomerates that suffocated its soul. People were mourning a business that had moved the dial. That had given them cult products, of course, but one that had educated and empowered them, and used its platform to stand up for issues its consumers cared about.

Anita Roddick was an activist who happened to be an extraordinary retailer. And that's exactly the kind of leadership we need now: business leaders who don't just chase profit but redefine its meaning. Who understand that commerce is not separate from conscience. Who recognise that the most powerful, relevant and enduring businesses of the future will be the ones that stand for something bigger than themselves. That are valuable because they are valued.

Because, in the end, the businesses that truly succeed won't just make money, they'll make a difference. And that is the greatest profit of all.

3. Trust and desire

Transparency, ethical sourcing, fair treatment of employees and sustainability aren't just 'nice to haves' any more – they're fundamental expectations. Trust is a business imperative.

But as much as people want to support so-called 'good businesses', they also crave beauty, aspiration and emotional connection. Desire is innate in humans. It's what makes people cherish certain brands whether that desire is sparked by the craftsmanship of a product, the story behind it or the way it makes them feel.

Consumerism isn't over; I would be a fool to suggest it was. The challenge for the fashion industry – for any industry built on consumption – is to create new forms of desirability that align with social and environmental sustainability.

I'm often approached by people telling me how great their daughters are. 'She only buys second-hand now, nothing new,' they'll proudly tell me. 'We popped into your Mary's Living and Giving shop the other day because she loves being able to say it's vintage.' Of course, I love hearing that. And sustainability is brilliant. But, sadly, the reality is there's still a huge population of young people who are caught in the sugar-hit cycle of new-new-new as they scroll-scroll-scroll. Platforms like Shein thrive despite questionable business practices, environmental toll and exploitative labour conditions. They make it so easy and so cheap to constantly feed the algorithm. The speed at which these young people are buying, returning and repurchasing . . . It's staggering.

Even people somewhere in the middle of these two extremes – not serial returners constantly seeking a new Friday-night outfit or status-seeking thrift hunters – have too much stuff. I can say that with confidence because we all have too much stuff. For decades we've been sold the lie that more stuff, the right stuff, will make us happy. But you know what? Creating too much stuff is harming not only our planet but contributing to the worst mental health crisis ever.

We are starting to break through. The conversation is shifting.

But it's a huge job, and it's one that we all have to take on together. At the heart of it is creating a new story, building a different mindset, redefining the status symbols at the heart of shopping. This isn't about demonising shopping. We will all carry on buying new things whether out of necessity or desire. But we must help people understand *why* they shop and *how* to make their choices better. We must make it modern to ask questions about where your stuff comes from. Make it cool. Make it sexy. And make sure people understand that mindful shopping is an exciting expression of who they are. Whether it's fashion, food, travel, or even tech, people still want things that make them feel good, that have status, that tell a story. But the definition of status has to keep shifting. It's no longer about just having *more*, it's about having *better*. That must feel like the modern and desirable choice.

And that's why the alchemy of trust and desire is so powerful: satisfying head and motivating heart. Accelerating the shift from unconscious demand to conscious demand.

4. Every corner of your business matters

In an age that demands radical transparency, today's businesses are like glass boxes: customers peer in, employees speak out, CEOs are on trial. In the context of the social web, every move can be trashed or celebrated for millions to witness. Businesses no longer control their own narrative or reputation. Every experience people have with you, both good and bad, can become a story. A business's internal culture matters as much as what's put out externally. As the motivational speaker Simon Sinek puts it: 'Customers will never love a company until the employees love it first.'

CEOs are the new celebrities – gaining traction and, in some cases, quasi-cabinet positions for their thought-leadership on business. Or being ousted when their bad behaviour or poor ethics are exposed. It can feel like a torture test for businesses. Lost in the fray, so many bury their heads in the sand, hide behind marketing or let the loudest person take over.

But to be truly generative, the opposite needs to happen. You need to dwell deeply, go into the very roots of your business and work out what you do, who you are and how people – all people – need to experience your business.

Because every single corner of your business matters: from the product to the team and operations. It's easy to have a bombastic vision, but if that vision doesn't match the reality felt by the customer or the employee, it won't resonate. It won't be trusted, and it certainly won't be desired. I often think about how the world's food chain would collapse should ants become extinct. Every single organism on Mother Earth would be affected. Businesses are no less exposed.

But on the flip side, magic happens when everything comes together, holistically and synergistically. From big acts to small gestures, it's about making people fall in love with what you do. And using all the new tools we have in our new digital ecosystem to connect, serve and inspire. Because when your customer believes in you, they want to spend time with you.

5. When in doubt, walk the shop floor

When things aren't working in retail, there is a famous adage: walk the shop floor. Because when you step onto the floor, you're not sitting in an office, removed from the pulse of your business. You're in the heart of it, where the action happens, where the truth of the brand lives.

No matter which brand I've worked with over the years, no matter which business, I've always made a point of stepping into their physical space – to really get under the skin of it. Because you can sit in endless meetings, listen to leaders talk passionately about their brand, their service, their customer experience, and you can see it all laid out in their charts – their mission, their philosophy, their values, all perfectly articulated. Then, one after-noon, you walk into their store, their hotel, their restaurant – the place where the brand truly lives, where people connect, react and respond – and, sometimes, what you see tells a very different story.

I remember the day they moved our offices out of Harvey Nichols to expand the fifth floor. It was just down the road, but it may as well have been miles away. I missed the rhythm of the store, the ease of running downstairs to speak to a buyer, the instinctive decisions we made. Should that fragrance counter move? Should that mannequin be repositioned? It was visceral, a connec-tion you could sense in your bones.

That's the magic of the shop floor. You don't just see when it's working – you feel it. The hum of conversation, the way the sun hits the entrance just as customers walk in, expectant and curious. It's those small yet significant moments. A career woman standing before a Gucci display, weighing up whether to invest in the jacket or the dress, and the quiet skill of a great sales assistant who guides her to the right choice, not just for her wardrobe but for her. The twenty-two-year-old coming in to buy a MAC lipstick and physically moving to the music, becoming a part of the scene. Retail isn't just about transactions; it's about energy, movement, emotion.

It's bigger than the sum of its parts. It's a living, breathing ecosystem.

And yet we've entered a time where so many brands have removed themselves from the action. Decisions are made remotely, far from the energy of the people who bring a business to life. That's why I believe every brand, even those built in the digital world, should have a physical space – a spiritual home, if you like, where the brand truly lives and breathes. Igniting the senses, enriching time, nourishing our souls. Because if the last few years have shown us anything, it's that community, connection and physical presence matter.

When I was a child I understood instinctively that 'shop' was a four-letter word that contained a world within it. A world of beautiful objects, however mundane they might seem. But more than that, when done right, a shop is not just a place to buy – it's a place to belong. Just as a business, done well, is about so much more than profit.

Great shops, like great businesses, bring people together. They galvanise communities and, with that connection, give us all a purpose and a rhythm, become part of our lives, our identities and our souls.

But great shops, no matter how good they are or how much we value their part in our community, only thrive with the choices we make. And in those choices lies our power – far greater than we might think.

'I shop, therefore I am' is a reminder each and every day that every pound we spend is a vote on the future we want to live in. And that is something we should never lose sight of.

Mary Portas OBE

Acknowledgements

Writing a memoir is not just an act of reflection, but a tribute to the many people who've walked beside me, shaped me, and made the journey rich with meaning. There are far too many of you to name – some whose presence was fleeting, whose names I may not recall today, but whose impact, however small, left a mark on the path I walked. You know who you are, and I thank you deeply. This book would not have been possible without the unwavering support of my brilliant team at Portas, the ever-insightful guidance from Hattie Brett and of course the remarkable team at Harvey Nichols – who not only helped build the business into what it is today, but who made me laugh and gave me some of the greatest, most memorable years of my life. My thanks to my agent, Cath Summerhayes, who I knew straight away was the one who would guide me through this process with laughter, wit, wisdom and absolute belief.

And finally to the exceptional team at Canongate – when I met them, I knew instantly that they shared the same energy, the same frequency, the same way of seeing the world as I do. I knew I was in the right hands – people who would understand my journey and help shape it into something even more meaningful. Thank you particularly to Helena Gonda for your trust, your partnership, and for holding the heart of this story so thoughtfully. This is as much yours as it is mine.